T

DIVIDED GOSPEL

The Consequences of Separating the Gospel from the Kingdom

THE DIVIDED GOSPEL

The Consequences of Separating the Gospel from the Kingdom

by

Dr. Joseph Mattera

Publisher—eGenCo

Powered by eGenCo Generation Culture Transformation
Specializing in publishing for generation culture change

eGenCo
824 Tallow Hill Road
Chambersburg, PA 17202, USA
Phone: 717-461-3436
Email: info@micro65.com
Website: www.micro65.com

facebook.com/egenbooks
egen.co/blog
twitter.com/egen_co
youtube.com/egenpub
pinterest.com/eGenDMP
instagram.com/egen.co

Publisher's Cataloging-in-Publication Data
Mattera, Joseph
The Divided Gospel. The Consequences of Separating the Gospel from the Kingdom.; by Dr. Joseph Mattera. Stephen Nance, editor.
94 pages cm.
ISBN: 978-1-68019-700-6 paperback
978-1-68019-798-3 ebook
978-1-68019-797-6 ebook
1. Religion. 2. Prosperity. 3. Leadership.
I. Title
2017964646

Cover Design by Kevin Lepp. (klmstudio.com)
Interior design by Versatile PreMedia Services

TABLE OF CONTENTS

Foreword

It would be difficult to overestimate the significance of the subject of this book. Joseph Mattera has clearly confronted one of the most stifling and destructive road blocks hindering the extension of God's Kingdom on earth today. Theology matters. Indeed, misinformed theology is one of Satan's most cherished weapons against God, His purposes, and His people. The separation or disconnect between the gospel of salvation and its relationship to God's emerging Kingdom on earth is right at the top of the list of most destructive ideas crippling the church and damaging the unsaved millions on earth.

As we know, salvation is the spiritual entry point into the Kingdom of God and the first step into an eternal process of transformation. This journey takes place in a social context both now and in the future, a social context best described as God's Kingdom—His realm of creation and oversight. A dynamic Kingdom in every way, it is currently filled with both spiritual family and obstacles. It is a dynamic Kingdom in every way, encompassing much more than the future only, as the apostle Paul so clearly reminds us in Colossians 1:13 where he says that at the point of our salvation we were "transferred to the Kingdom of His beloved Son." Though we still await His future earthly appearance and the next phase in the eternal Kingdom drama, to deny the newness of His Kingdom life in the present is more than heretical—it is spiritual theft. This heresy robs its victims of the joy of laboring with Christ today as the Holy Spirit partners with us in the extension of His live-giving Kingdom in this present hour.

Postponing the reality of the Kingdom until we reach heaven robs God, ourselves, and humanity as a whole of the existential current presence of God's Kingdom that even as we speak is dethroning the kingdoms of this world. If "the just shall live by faith" (Hebrews 10:38), then God's Kingdom is extended by faith. If it doesn't exist for us now on earth, it will not come through us. This is deep water to plumb the depths of, but the Kingdom comes through us because it is self-consciously in us. Without the self-consciousness of "owned truth," there is no such thing as faith. All of Christ's miracles rested on the faith He perceived resting within people. No faith, no miracle; no newness, no extension of Christ's Kingdom through us. If there is no extension of His Kingdom here on earth through us now, our praying of the Lord's Prayer is both faithless and meaningless. "Thy kingdom come, Thy will be done in earth as it is in heaven" (Matthew 6:10) becomes mere religious talk.

In this book Joe Mattera has summarily enumerated a host of common fallacies that are faith-killers to the Kingdom. He is gifted at doing so both in what he says and writes. Cutting these spiritual pygmies off at the knees is a service to God and an opportunity to bring joyful fruit to those who have been liberated. This book, accessible to many because of its brevity, may be a game-changer for significant numbers of people. I thank Joe for his obedience to God and the service he has rendered to his readers. Please enjoy the journey and pass it on to others! Thy Kingdom come through you…

Dennis Peacocke, Summer 2017

Introduction

Truly, the greatest discovery I ever made in the Bible was when my eyes were opened to understand how the Gospel relates to the Kingdom of God! When this happened in 1995, I had been preaching for seventeen years an individualistic approach to the Gospel that reduced it conceptually to deal only in terms of individual salvation. What was missing was the societal and systemic impact the Gospel is supposed to have, which is embedded throughout Scripture.

One of the things that triggered my conversion to the Gospel of the Kingdom was something I noticed as I studied American church history: the pre-Civil War church preached the Kingdom of God, but the post-war church moved away from it. The Kingdom message influenced the pre-war church to deal with societal issues such as slavery, child labor laws, the dangers of alcohol, and more. The post-war church started to focus merely on the Rapture, the last days, and escaping the earth instead of engaging it. This escapist focus resulted in the church essentially abandoning culture, which opened the door to the secular humanists taking over every major institution of higher learning by the 1920s.

One generation later, in the 1960s, this entrenched humanist presence bore bitter fruit in the form of the Cultural and Sexual Revolution. Many of the students and activists of that era eventually became our politicians, social and cultural icons, and academics, and their pervasive influence radically altered the worldview of many Americans. Consequently, in recent years we have witnessed the legalization of abortion, the arrival of transgender bathroom laws, the re-definition of marriage, and other secular progressive policies. For more details regarding why the post-Civil War church abandoned the Gospel of the Kingdom, see my book Ruling in the Gates.[1]

The Kingdom of God is *not* the church!

Aside from American church history, I also discovered that the primary theme of the New Testament–and of the preaching of John the Baptist, Jesus, and the apostle Paul–was the Kingdom of God. (See, for example, Matt. 3:2; 4:17; Mk. 1:15; Acts 20:25; 28:31.) Also, the Gospel Jesus preached to the poor resulted in systemic change that positively impacted cities and nations, not just individuals. (See Isa. 61:1-4, which Jesus quoted in Lk. 4:18-19).

When we divide the good news of Christ from the message of His Kingdom, the result is an individualistic mindset in the church that can easily lead to narcissism and self-focus. This is because a kingdom implies the King's domain, which includes the systems of the created order such as economics, politics, education, business, family, science, history, psychology, the arts, and all the spheres and/or cultural mountains. Detaching the Gospel from these systems of the Kingdom strips the church of its original assignment of stewarding the earth, leaving it with nothing to focus on except individual redemption and hope. Conversely, when the church lifts whole cities and nations with the influence of the Kingdom (see Isa. 58:12), more people will be won for Christ anyway!

The following chapters summarize how the church lost its influence in the culture from dividing the Gospel from the Kingdom of God—and how we can get it back.

---

1 Joseph Mattera, *Ruling in the Gates: Preparing the Church to Transform Cities.* (Lake Mary, FL: Creation House Press, a part of Strang Communications Company, 2003).

Chapter One

The church lost its purpose of stewarding the earth according to Genesis 1:28.

> *And God said to them, "Be fruitful and multiply and fill the earth and subdue it and have dominion over the fish of the sea and over the birds of the heavens and over every living thing that moves on the earth" (Genesis 1:28).*

I believe the "Cultural Mandate" found in Genesis 1:28 is the key passage that unlocks the rest of the Bible. Without this original covenant given to Adam, we cannot understand the purpose of the church, the resurrection of Christ, and the purpose of the second bodily return of Christ. In fact, until we understand this first covenant that many call the "Cultural Mandate," we cannot properly understand every subsequent covenant found in Scripture. Since this was the first covenant after God finished His six days of Creation, every other covenant receives its substance from this first covenant.

For example, in Genesis 9:1- 2, we see that even after the fall of Adam, God repeated the Cultural Mandate almost verbatim to Noah. In Genesis chapter 12:1-3, after the earth was populated, God told Abram (Abraham) that in him all the nations of the earth would be blessed, which shows us that God's will was to continue the mandate of influencing the whole earth. In Genesis 17:5-7, God told Abraham that out of his loins kings and princes would emerge, and, in Genesis 22:17-18, that his offspring would possess the gates of their enemies.

Having influence in the gates equates to having influence in politics and culture because the gates were a metaphor in Scripture for the places of power in a city and nation; they were also literally where the kings and elders of the city made policy decisions. None of this language could be understood without the original covenant of creation called the Cultural Mandate (Gen. 1:28).

Going further, we see that even in the Mosaic covenant God called His people to be the head and not the tail, and to be above and not beneath (Deut. 28;10-13). In Psalm 2:8-9, God promised to give His Son all the nations of the earth as His inheritance. In Psalm 110:1-3, God told His Son to sit at His right hand until His enemies become His footstool. This may imply that Jesus will not return bodily to the earth a second time until there is a strong Kingdom witness throughout the earth.

In the New Testament, 1 Corinthians 15:45 calls Jesus the "last Adam," which shows us that He came to fulfill the Cultural Mandate given to the first Adam in Genesis 1:28. This gives more clarity to why Jesus called His followers to disciple all nations (Matt. 28:19). All of this illustrates that we cannot understand either the first or second testament of the Bible without starting with Genesis 1:28, which frames all subsequent covenants. Consequently, the Cultural Mandate becomes our interpretive grid to understand not only every other covenant, but also every other passage of Scripture. The Gospel of the Kingdom that both Jesus and Paul preached was the continuation of this original covenant, which is why Jesus commanded His followers to disciple whole nations, not just individual ethnics (see Matt. 28:19-20). Hence, if we are called to disciple whole nations then we are in essence called to manage planet earth and steward the world. When we disconnect the Gospel, or the good news, from the Kingdom we hinder Christ-followers from understanding their call to influence and lead in all of life, not just church life. Separating the Gospel from the Kingdom separates Christ from His Kingdom in our theology, which affects the way we preach to our congregations.

Instead of proclaiming the good news of the reign of God through Christ, we are left with an individualistic gospel whose only promise is of experiencing heaven in the next life. This can lead Christ-followers into mysticism. When we take away the call of the believer to steward the earth, we hinder our ability to make disciples who will be the salt of the earth and the light of the world. We also weaken the church's call to be an equipping center to fill the earth with believers in every facet of society, to His glory!

Without the reign of God on earth as our focus, we are left with little more than merely experiencing God during Sunday church services, thus limiting the Kingdom of God to operating only within four walls of the church building for two hours every Sunday. This brings us to our next chapter.

Chapter Two

The church tended to become narcissistic and focused on self-fulfillment.

"Whoever finds his life will lose it, and whoever loses his life for my sake will find it" (Matthew 10:39).

When we disconnect the Gospel from an obligation to care for and steward the planet, we are left with a Jesus who came only to redeem us for our own sake. Unfortunately, this has devolved over many generations into a contemporary gospel message that is more about self-fulfillment than serving others. The sad result is self-focused congregations that only come to church for individual blessings and good feelings. This self-centered expectation has shaped much of the preaching today in America and beyond, which often dwells on how God can make us happy, provide for our needs, and give us a blessed life. Although this has some biblical truth, it becomes erroneous when we make it our primary focus.

The worst part is that instead of exalting the triune God, we exalt the false "trinity" of "I, me, my." Without a greater purpose for life, Christians begin to act like the world in regards to living for stability, happiness, and self-fulfillment—rather than losing their lives in order to see others saved. The gospel of self-fulfillment and narcissism is about us, not Him! The narcissistic gospel is about seeking blessings more than seeking the Blesser.

Since the dawn of the "positive thinking" message of Norman Vincent Peale in the mid-20th century, an avalanche of preachers have followed his lead, proclaiming their own versions of this "health and wealth" prosperity gospel, or "name it and claim it," along with various other modes of motivational preaching. Although this positive message extracts truth from Scripture and has great merit when properly applied, if isolated outside the whole counsel of God, it can be misleading and even disheartening for adherents who fail to see their dreams come true. Furthermore, when the objective is "self-fulfillment," this message often reduces the Gospel of Christ to nothing more than appeasing the narcissistic dreams of half-baked Christians.

Although Scripture teaches us to focus our thoughts upon things that are true, noble, and lovely, that instruction occurs in the context of dealing with relational conflict and financial challenges. That is to say, there is no denial of life's challenges but an appeal to trust God intentionally in our thought life during these situations.

In the remainder of this chapter, I want to summarize my concerns by enumerating nine errors evident in the gospel of self-fulfillment:

1. The cross of Christ is absent.

I have read many motivational Christian and secular books from all genres, and the one glaring truth that is missing is the cross of Christ. Jesus plainly told His followers that they had to take up their cross and follow Him (Matt. 16: 24). Therefore, we are called to appropriate the power of His finished work on the cross to our own self-centered desires so we can fulfill His will. This cuts straight across "hyper grace" preachers who teach that the Gospel message of the cross is not relevant to the church. (See Romans 6 and Galatians 2:19 -20 to learn what the apostle Paul taught the church with regard to applying the cross to their own flesh.)

The reason why the cross is absent from the gospel of self-fulfillment is because it is antithetical to its essence. The cross rebuts the notion of attempting to live a life without suffering as it also controverts the notion of living a life based on self-fulfillment. In reality, God calls us to do many things that we do not like and/or that do not grant us great happiness. (Changing diapers in the middle of the night, loving others unconditionally, laboring in the ministry without appreciation or without seeing immediate fruit, et al.) Paul even said that he did not count his life of any value so that he might finish the ministry the Lord gave him (Acts 20:24). I have found that when you try to empower believers without preaching the cross, they invariably will attempt to serve God in their own strength—and fail miserably.

2. It empowers egocentric dreams.

One popular mantra in today's world is, "You can be anything you want to be." And another, "All your dreams can come true." The reality, however, is that not all of our dreams and desires are God-given and/or grounded in reality. Reality includes self-awareness regarding one's own natural ability and talent. When we tell people they can be anything they want to be, we set them up for disillusionment if their desire is not rooted in God.

3. There is rarely a mention of sin.

Although I have read dozens of motivational books, I do not remember reading anything substantive about the consequences of sinful living. These books and their exponents seem only to focus on "positive things" and rarely mention how the practice of conscious sin can derail a person's calling. Unfortunately, this gives believers the impression that living a holy life is inconsequential to fulfilling their purpose. Of course, Scripture plainly teaches otherwise (see 1 Cor. 10:6-14; Heb. 3-4).

4. People are not taught to admit personal weakness.

Second Corinthians chapters 11 and 12 detail how the apostle Paul had no issue with bragging about his weaknesses. This grounded Paul and his readers in reality and helped them understand how believers need to depend upon the power of Christ to fulfill their calling. Unfortunately, many in the "self-fulfillment" camp rarely admit their weaknesses in public because it goes against their public personification of perfection, personal victory, and success.

5. It promotes the fallacy of no limitations.

Another lesson I have learned is that I have personal limitations. Understanding my natural and spiritual strengths, proclivities, and weaknesses helps me focus. I do not waste my time trying to walk outside the lane of my assignment and abilities. This flies in the faces of those who take Paul out of context and cite, "I can do all things through him [Christ] who strengthens me" (Phil. 4:13). In this passage Paul was not referring to accomplishing whatever he wanted, but fulfilling God's call in spite of his financial challenges. Read Philippians 4:10-13 for the full context.

6. Failure and pain are not part of the process (so say the self-fulfillment crowd).

Another life lesson I have learned is that I cannot avoid pain in the process of fulfilling my purpose in Christ. Sometimes pain is self-inflicted and can be avoided, but oftentimes it is out of our control because it has to do with the deleterious actions of others. However, like the Lord Jesus, the apostle Paul, every Kingdom leader, every Kingdom citizen—every Christ-follower, in other words—likely will suffer a form of betrayal from one or more of their close associates, friends, and even family. Also, sometimes we make wrong decisions in life that cause us to fail in a particular endeavor. The only person who does not fail is the person who never attempts to do anything challenging.

The key to success is not to avoid failure but to "fall forward" and learn from the experience. Unfortunately, many motivational speakers and books are not honest with their followers regarding the inevitability of pain and failure. Even many faith teachers have taught that we should always go from "victory to victory" without laying out the challenging process between the beginning and end of an endeavor.

7. The goal is often happiness.

Many come to church seeking happiness, but happiness is not God's top priority for us in this life. Our highest calling is to know God and obey Him, not seek a life of self-fulfillment and pleasure (see Phil. 3:3-12). I have discovered, ironically, that the unhappiest people I know are the ones whose primary motivation in life is to be happy! This is because every time something happens that goes against their craving for happiness, they become unhappy! The happiest people you will ever meet are those who live to serve God and others. Truly, they are the happiest people on earth.

8. It is individualistic.

Another grave error of the gospel of self-fulfillment is the fact that it is based upon individual fulfillment and destiny. In Scripture, there is no such thing as an individual earthly vision, mission, purpose, and destiny. Everything we do is interrelated with other people because we are all part of the same Body of Christ (see1 Cor.12:12-27). For example, the Old Testament was written to the nation of Israel and the New Testament was written for the benefit of the church. Most promises and passages cannot be properly interpreted and applied outside of the context of these two entities, Israel and the church. Of course, the major exception to this is when every person stands before the judgment seat of Christ. There we will stand as individuals without the ability to use another person or situation as a scapegoat (see 2 Cor. 5:10).

9. It doesn't teach the whole counsel of God.

The apostle Paul said he was free from the blood of all men because he taught them the whole counsel of God (Acts 20:26-27). When we only accentuate certain truths to the exclusion of other truths in the Bible we are guilty of reflecting the wrong image of God and His Word. Many preachers of the gospel of self-fulfillment focus on the goodness and love of God to the exclusion of His righteousness, holiness, and justice. Scripture teaches us that righteousness and justice are the foundation of His throne (or rule); hence, when we exclude this side of God we are left without a divine foundation. After all, we cannot fully appreciate the love of God for us in Christ until we also understand the righteous wrath of God against sin, and we cannot understand God's goodness until we grasp how He loved and saved us in spite of His holy hatred against sin. When we preach only the love and goodness of God, we can give the impression that God winks at sin and that believers can live any way they want without fear of divine retribution. This opposes the passages in Scripture that warn all people, including believers, that we will reap what we sow (see Gal. 6:7-9; Eph. 5:2-6).

I have read dozens of motivational books, and probably will read many more, because they contain biblical truths regarding positive thinking, faith, and the maximization of our God-given abilities and talents. However, to confine my reading to this genre alone would be unhealthy because it often accentuates certain attributes of God's nature and character and excludes others. When we only expose ourselves to one genre of teaching, we become unbalanced and eventually will find out that our belief does not correspond with real life experience.

Chapter Three

Biblical prosperity became about individual blessing instead of spreading God's covenant on the earth.

> *"But remember the LORD your God, for it is he who gives you the ability to produce wealth, and so confirms his covenant..." (Deuteronomy8:18 NIV)*

This passage in Deuteronomy teaches us that God has given believers the power to create wealth so His covenant can be confirmed upon the earth. This obligates us to connect our finances with Kingdom purposes instead of the present prosperity gospel, which is primarily about having nice cars and homes, and living a life of luxury and convenience! Also, much has been much written in recent years about the Christian's role in producing wealth on the earth. There are several misconceptions in the church regarding prosperity and wealth creation that need adjustment for us to have biblical balance and integrity, as well as experience transformation in our families, communities, and nations. Most of these misconceptions arise from the ignorance we have regarding the Gospel of the Kingdom.

The first misconception is that prosperity is automatic for all Christians. Although God desires prosperity for all His children (see 3 John 2), nowhere in the Bible does it say that saints automatically are blessed financially simply because they are saved. The Book of Proverbs is replete with principles of wealth creation that deal with activating the laws of sowing and reaping, wisdom, and integrity to produce financial wealth–principles that redeemed people do not necessarily practice after their conversion to Christ (see Prov. 6:6-8; 10:4-5; Gal. 6:7; 2 Cor. 9:6).

A second misconception is that God only claims ten percent of our finances. The error is that God claims only ten percent of our finances and that we can do what we want with the remaining ninety percent of our money. The truth of the matter is that God claims *all* of our money; the tithe is simply a minimum of ten percent that should go directly to the ecclesial realm for the spread of the Gospel. Luke 14:33 teaches that disciples of Christ are to relinquish ownership of one hundred percent of their possessions because we are merely His stewards of what we own when we make Him our Lord. "The earth is the LORD's and the fullness thereof" (Psalm 24:1).

The Bible not only teaches us to tithe, but also to get out of burdensome debt that causes a depreciation of our wealth (Prov. 22:7); to invest wisely (Matt. 25:27); to be shrewd in our business dealings (Lk. 16:8); to save for our future generations (Prov. 13:22); and to create business plans (Lk. 14:28). The Bible also teaches us against co-signing for those we do not know well (Prov. 11:15) and to deal honestly with others (Prov. 11:1). So you see, how we steward one hundred percent of our money will determine how wealthy we will become, not just how we steward ten percent of our money.

A third misconception is that God wants us prosperous so we can be happy. God tells us clearly in Deuteronomy 8:18 that the primary purpose of wealth is so we can finance the spread of His covenant on the earth. The deal is this: If we seek first His Kingdom with our finances, then He will give us what we desire anyway (see Matt. 6:33; Ps. 37:4). Biblical prosperity has more to do with pleasing the Lord and making Him happy than obtaining wealth so we can experience personal happiness.

A fourth misconception is that all Christians are called to be very wealthy. Although God has called the corporate Body of Christ to leverage great wealth, not all individual Christians, or even pastors, can handle large amounts of money. God will only give His people individually that which they are able to properly manage and administrate (see Deut. 7:22). Taking it a step further, some pastors and churches could even be damaged if certain billionaires came into their churches and gave them their tithes. The tithe on a billion dollars is $100 million. How many small to mid-sized churches can properly steward that kind of wealth? Also, how many people who have won the lottery have kept their wealth, health, and family? Jesus came to give every person an abundant life (see Jn. 10:10), but not every person has been given the same amount of talents (see Matt. 25:14-15). Some have been given five talents, some two, and some one, all according to their God-given ability and assignment. Hence, not everyone in your local church is called to be a multimillionaire.

The fifth misconception is that prosperity is the right of all who are in Christ. It is high time that we in the Body of Christ move from a "rights-centered" Gospel, which has its historical roots in the American fight for independence and Jeffersonian preaching, to a "stewardship-centered" Gospel, in which we view our gifts, calling, and resources as a responsibility to serve and bless others—not something handed to us because we have the "right" to it as a Christian. Matthew 25 shows the great balance in this because it talks both about the command to properly invest our talents for an appreciation of assets that results in multiplication, and then illustrates that the reason for the talents is so we can feed the hungry, clothe the naked, heal the sick, visit the prisoners, and be hospitable to the strangers and aliens (Matt. 25:14-46). This and other passages clearly show that the primary purpose of wealth is a matter of stewardship to serve humanity, not a matter of our "right" because we are Christians.

A sixth misconception is that wealth creation is the key to breaking the spirit of poverty. Creating more money has never been the main key to breaking poverty. According to

Genesis 1:27-28, the church must produce strong and stable marriages and biblically trained children, which is the first key to replenishing the earth, subduing our enemies, and having dominion (great influence). True prosperity is never only about money. Wealth creation is merely one of the by-products for people who walk in their assignment with integrity, humility, focus, and diligence—all of which should be modeled at home by parents long before their children reach adulthood.

A seventh misconception is that churches only need more money to influence and transform their communities. The easiest way for a local church to leverage great power and influence and transform a community is by loving and serving their community and city. When a local church has an army of paid and unpaid volunteers who educate at-risk children, help young people excel in the arts, sports, and life skills, provide much-needed services for the poor, the fatherless, and aliens, and partner with community leaders and elected officials, then God's favor rests on that church. This opens up more doors and buildings than money could buy! Community and business leaders will do whatever it takes to allow that church to have any facility and resource they need to further bless their community.

This was the primary method the early church used to spread the Gospel. Instead of purchasing buildings, they filled everyone else's buildings (except the pagan temples) with loving, sacrificial Christians who risked their lives to care for the diseased, nurse abandoned babies, and bury rotting corpses left in the town garbage dumps. Truly, when the church goes after those nobody else wants, God will give them those everybody wants! Taking a city does not just happen with a top-down approach of amassing wealth and speaking to power; it also involves a bottom-up approach with effective, compassionate ministries.

The eighth misconception is that it only takes faith to release prosperity. Those of us who "named and claimed" prosperity found out the hard way that we not only have to speak faith and think positively, but also have to read books on wealth creation, work hard, and receive proper coaching from those who have already gone financially where we feel called to go. It is not just about faith and it is not just about sowing money; it is about working hard and learning how to get, how to manage what we get, how to save, how to invest money where it appreciates and multiplies the most, and how to disciple and empower others so they too can learn how to produce wealth for the Kingdom.

Finally, the ninth misconception is that prosperity only relates to our present. Most preaching today regarding prosperity only has an "I," "me," and "my" emphasis, which is a one-generation approach. God revealed Himself not only as the God of Abraham, but also as the God of Isaac and Jacob (Ex. 3:6) because He has called us to plan for at least three generations in everything we do. I pray that the days will come to an end when the preaching is only on individualistic topics like, "How you can write your own ticket with God," or "How you can receive your miracle"! Those of us maturing in the faith message and prosperity realize that God has called us to think corporately in terms of our present and future the same way He does (see Ex. 20:5-6; 1 Ch. 16:15). We realize that God will transfer the wealth of the wicked only to those righteous who leave an inheritance for their grandchildren (see Prov. 13:22).

After all, most of the money today is in "old" money, not "new" money (with the exception of Bill Gates and some others who have blazed the technological trail in this present information age), which means that wealth was accumulated over the course of multiple generations and kept in families (the Rockefellers, for example). This is one reason why the Fifth Commandment (see Eph. 6:3) tells us that if we honor our father and mother it will go well for us and we will live long on the earth. Those who only think in terms of their present life are no better than economist John Maynard

Keynes, who influenced the present American economic strategy with debt financing. He and those like him were not thinking of future generations but only about indulging their lust for the temporal present. May God deliver the church from such a mindset!

Chapter Four

The church promoted an individual rather than a corporate mindset.

"For the body is not one member, but many"
(1 Corinthians 12:14 KJV).

The Bible is no less than God's personal love letter to individuals, but it is also much more: a legally binding covenantal document meant to disciple nations. The Old Testament was written to the nation of Israel (individuals could not apply the covenant if they were outside of the camp) and the New Testament was written to the church. Presently, we have many believers with an individualistic mindset who attempt to interpret and apply God's promises and blessings in the Bible to themselves, in spite of the fact they are not committed to a local community of faith–a concept completely foreign to both the Hebrew mindset and the original intent of Scripture!

Their individualistic mindset also goes against the Hebraic corporate mindset of the Scriptures, resulting in preaching, teaching, and theological positions that force onto the biblical text meanings and interpretations that are not in accord with the inspired writings of the authors. Look at the Book of Acts, for example. Luke, the inspired writer, did not provide biographical sketches of any of the apostles. His main purpose was not to highlight individual lives or accomplishments, but to focus on the corporate mission. Today's church, by and large, has reversed this; the primary focus now is on the individual Christian superstar rather than on the community of faith.

Without the Gospel of the Kingdom, we are left with good news that applies merely to individual believers. Combining the Gospel with the Kingdom, however, gives us a holistic approach that is less self-focused and more corporate-minded—and this shift in focus has vast implications! God knows what is best for us to fulfill our purpose and walk in spiritual and emotional health. Scripture plainly teaches that individual believers thrive spiritually the most when they learn how to incorporate their lives into the context of a local faith community.

Nowadays, it is very common, even for people serving in leadership positions, to come to life-altering conclusions without including mature leaders in their process. This is the individualistic mindset at work, informed more by cultural norms than by adherence to Scripture. To better understand this difference in thinking, consider the following contrasts between the individualistic and (Hebraic) corporate mindsets.

The corporate mindset is about we; the individual is about me.

I think it was John Maxwell who said, "There is no 'I' in the word team." Those who walk in the Hebraic mindset of Scripture understand that every decision we make affects not just ourselves, but everyone around us. The most effective people in the world and church today are those who understand and work with teams of people and/or a community with common goals to accomplish specific tasks.

Biblically, people were sent by the church. Today, most just go out on their own.

In Scripture, the church deliberately sent believers out to fulfill their mission in Christ (see Acts 13:1-2). Paul even asked, "And how can they preach unless they are sent?" (Rom. 10:15 NIV). Nowadays, because of the individualistic mindset, this sending process is almost unheard of in the church. The common practice today is, "I feel led by the Lord to leave the church," or "I feel led to do this or that." Hence, people come to their own conclusions regarding their life and ministry without any pastoral input, and then inform their spiritual leaders of their decision. Because of the preponderance of individualism in the culture, when a leader teaches the biblical protocol of "being sent," people sometimes accuse them of trying to control them or hold them back. (Of course, controlling leaders can indeed, and often do use the Bible for their own selfish ends, which is unfortunate for everyone.) However, being "sent" instead of just "went" serves as a protection that provides extra layers of checks and balances. When someone starts a ministry and/or a church, the number one question they should be asked is, "Who sent you." If their only answer is, "God sent me," then they may be making big mistakes regarding protocol and timing, which may call their motivation into question.

Biblically, believers received counsel from the elders. Today, believers merely Google for input.

Presently, the widespread availability of social media has enabled many people to become self-ordained "experts" just because they can do their own research on Google. However, Google cannot replace godly, wise input from mature leaders who know the Scriptures and can discern the mind of God. Furthermore, when making life-altering decisions, we often need more than mere data; we need to understand various perspectives that can only come from another person. Now, virtually anyone can declare himself or herself an authority on any subject once they have researched it online for an hour. Such a mindset is both arrogant and naïve. It reeks of rugged individualism and is a dangerous way to live.

Biblically, it's about corporate destiny. Today, it's about individual destiny.

Scripture teaches us that when there is no vision the people perish (see Prov. 29:18). This passage illustrates corporate vision since it affects many people, not just one person, or a few. Although Scripture is replete with passages dealing with corporate destiny, much of the preaching today has to do with fulfilling individual destiny. However, when folks living in the New Testament era read an epistle, it was while they were assembled together as a congregation. This letter was read out loud to the church. Hence, they interpreted the Scripture corporately rather than individualistically, because that was the context of their experience.

Today, it seems as though everybody has their own study Bible, and they tend to forget that both the first and second testaments were written to be read in the hearing of an assembled community (see Rom. 10:17). Of course, we do well to remember that for the first 1500 years of church history there were no printing presses and few, if any, had their own Bible. The fact that we have our own Bibles today lends itself more easily to the mindset of individualism than it did in most of the days of the church's existence. The two testaments together span was about 3500 years of biblical history before the printing press was introduced.

Biblically, the church is a family of families. Today, the church is for individual (existential) experiences.

Scripture teaches us (1 Corinthians 12:12-13) that when we are saved we are automatically baptized into the Body of Christ and made to partake of one body. Thus, even in our individual salvation experience we cannot detach our life from the Body of Christ. In spite of this truth, most people attend church services today for an existential experience they perceive will benefit them individually and personally. Consequently, our present culture has reduced the biblical concept of the Body of Christ to individual subjective experiences in which a believer picks and chooses, and enters and leaves, local churches merely for a "spiritual" experience. Yet, the church is primarily a family of families; Paul even calls it "the household of faith" in Galatians 6:10. Identifying the church as family has vast implications for today's believers and churches. In a biological family people are not together just to have good experiences, but to serve each other, love each other, and work together in spite of any disagreements they may have. It is the same with the household of faith. We need to view the church organically and conceptually as a family, not merely a gathering place for good spiritual feelings.

Biblically, we are to pray as a corporate body. Today, we only pray positioned as individuals.

Jesus taught us to pray, "Our Father in heaven…" (Matt. 6:9), but most Christians today pray "My Father…." In the Old Testament, both Daniel (9:5) and Nehemiah (1:6-7) prayed to God and said "we have sinned," thus identifying corporately with the sin of their faith community even though they themselves were not guilty of such transgressions. These examples clearly show us not only how to pray, but also how these biblical leaders viewed themselves in the context of their spiritual family. The success of their faith community was their success, and the sins of their faith community were their sins. Presently, when typical believers sees something they don't agree with in their local church, they immediately detach themselves from it, leave the church, and talk badly about their (former) faith family. Most believers today have very little understanding of how God views believers together as one body.

Biblically, each of us individually is a son of God; that is our identity, in part. Collectively, we are "sons of God," part of a greater whole, God's corporate son, whom He is conforming into the likeness of His only begotten Son (see Rom. 8:14-19, 29-30).

My prayer is that we will consider carefully how much the Body of Christ today has incorporated a culturally induced, individualistic mindset and lost much of our corporate sensibility. Unless we change, this mindset will limit our capacity to edify the church and cap our effectiveness in His Kingdom.

Chapter Five

The church won hearts but lost the minds of the next generation.

"Jesus replied: 'Love the Lord your God with all your heart and with all your soul and with all your mind'" (Matthew 22:37 NIV).

Ever since the apostle Paul preached the Gospel to the intellectual elite on Mars Hill in Athens, we understand that Christianity involves loving God with the mind, not just the heart (see Acts 17). Paul said he became all things to all people so that he may win some (1Cor. 9:22). That is what he did when he preached to the philosophers on Mars Hill. Rather than preaching from the Hebrew Scriptures, he quoted from their own poets and used their own religious background to present the Gospel in a palatable way they could understand.

In contrast, when Paul preached the Gospel to the Jews he reasoned from the Scriptures and didn't refer to the contemporary literature of the surrounding culture and/or nature. (See Acts chapters 13-17 to learn more about Paul's divergent approach in presenting the Gospel.)

Nowadays, although the church is getting more acclimated to the Gospel of the Kingdom along with the seven-mountain mandate, most believers still are only comfortable having conversations amongst themselves. Most believers do not have a biblical worldview or life philosophy effective enough to give a presentation of the hope of the Gospel in the secular arena (see 1 Pet. 3:15). Hence, the church has been relegated to having conversations within the four walls of a building on Sunday and getting excited with great preaching, but never applying their faith in the public square.

The consequence of this is the evangelical church has missed multiple huge opportunities to shift the culture after massive revivals brought thousands into the local church.

A case in point is the 1960's "Jesus Movement," when hundreds of thousands of hippies and other young people were saved and added to the church. Unfortunately, while the church may have won their hearts, the world won over their minds!

While we adapted the church culture to embrace these young people by dressing more casually, becoming less religious, and allowing Christian rock music and electric worship music in order to appeal to them, we never discipled their minds with the biblical worldview regarding political theory, economics, philosophy, education, and biblical ethics. Consequently, many of these young Christians continued to live by the humanistic worldview they learned in secular universities, including some who went on to become present-day cultural leaders.

Our current moral dilemma is not the result of a lack of Christians in politics; it is a lack of biblical thinking in politics and policy. Many of the youth of the 1960's humanistic revolution are today national leaders who have shifted our society towards a secular worldview that marginalizes Christianity! Many so-called boomer generation Christian leaders have led the charge to reduce faith to the private sphere, away from the theater of culture.

Unfortunately, for the past fifty years the church has been asleep at the wheel in regards to cultural engagement. If the church had discipled those saved in the Jesus Movement of the 60s and 70s with a biblical worldview and taught them how to apply their faith to culture, our nation today would have an ethos closer to biblical ethics. Of course, the moral dilemma we are experiencing today is nothing new.

Nowadays, there is a small but growing movement among Christian leaders (including myself) who are attempting to apply the Bible to contemporary culture so the church can function as salt and light and disciple the nations.

The early church grappled with the same issue of being biblical but relevant to contemporary society. Let's examine some of this Christian history to get a better idea of how the early church adapted evangelism to their changing culture and context.

The Early Church in Its Culture[2]

Soon after the first generation of its birth, the church faced the need to proclaim the Gospel in terms intelligent people could understand. Greek philosophy was the language of the intelligentsia during this time period. To some in the church, like Tertullian, being relevant to society in these terms was a compromise with the world. He said, "What has Athens to do with Jerusalem?" Thus, through the centuries the church has always grappled with the tension between "detachment and involvement" and "separation from the world yet penetration of the world." This has caused divisions in the church because "witness to some is compromise to others."

The first Christian apologist to successfully preach Christianity in the language of the philosopher was Justin, who preached while clad in the garb of the typical philosopher. Around 180 A.D. Pantaenus established a school of Christian Gnosticism in Alexandria and lectured there on Christianity as the true philosophy. His teaching was called gnostic because it asked the big questions of meaning, but it was Christian because it retained orthodox answers. Clement was a student of his for 20 years before he became his successor. Clement was not only versed in the Scriptures but in the knowledge of his time, including Greek philosophy

2 Content of this section is summarized from Bruce L. Shelley, *Church History in Plain Language, Updated 2nd Edition*. (Nashville: Thomas Nelson Publishers, 1982, 1995), 78-86.

and classical literature. He understood the problems and questions of the young who came to him from all over the empire and enrolled in his school.

Clement's goal was not to win arguments but people to Christ as an apostle to the Hellenistic world. Clement viewed philosophy as a schoolmaster to lead Greeks to Christ in the same way the Law of Moses led Jews to Messiah. The results of Clement's ministry were astounding! From this point on, Greek thinking united with Christian thought and influenced all the great saints, theologians, and church councils to come. A persecution forced Clement to flee and leave the school in the hands of a brilliant 18-year-old named Origen.

Origen was an even more successful leader than Clement, whose influence spread all over the empire with his exhaustive writings, including a vast study of six versions of the Old Testament entitled the *Hexapla,* scores of commentaries, and hundreds of sermons. He also introduced the mode of biblical interpretation known as allegorical interpretation of Scripture, which teaches that there are three levels of interpretation of Scripture: a literal interpretation, a moral application to the soul, and an allegorical or spiritual sense which refers to the mysteries of the Christian faith. Although known as a Christian philosopher, Origen felt that his main calling was the exposition of the Scriptures. His enormous work enabled intelligent Christians to believe the Bible. Origen was also among the first systematic theologians of the church, and was the first theologian to set forth the whole intellectual framework of the Christian faith. He realized that if Christianity were to succeed in shaping civilizations it must justify itself to the intellect as well as to the heart of mankind.

***

So we see that the issue of contemporary apologetics was something many great saints of old grappled with. Relevant apologetics is always in flux and based upon the demographics, ethos, and ideological backgrounds of the surrounding communities.

When we separate the Gospel from the Kingdom, we think only about escaping the earth rather than engaging it. Hence, we tend to park our brains at the door of the church assemblies. Only a Kingdom-focused church will grapple with culture the way the early church once did.

In conclusion, when we connect the Gospel to the Kingdom we are also compelled to use our intellect—not just our spirit—when applying the Scriptures to culture. Until we believers learn to love God with our minds as well as our hearts, we will never convert the preponderance of the next generation to Christ.

Chapter Six

The church missed the opportunity to disciple many emerging leaders of our nation.

> *"...the things you have heard from me in the presence of many witnesses entrust to faithful men who will be able to teach others also" (2 Timothy 2:2).*

If Steve Jobs were alive today as an eighteen-year-old and visited a typical evangelical church (to connect his creative imagination with his Creator), he would probably be disappointed and leave! Rather than messages on the importance of stewarding the earth, he probably would hear only sermons related to heaven, personal fulfillment, and the rapture of the church, leaving him to conclude that the church has no relevant message to offer emerging cultural creative's like himself.

Unfortunately, I believe this scenario is played out week after week in our churches, causing us to miss countless opportunities to attract the greatest leaders of our generation who have an innate desire for cultural engagement but are turned off by escapist theology. Separating the Gospel from the Kingdom creates a domino effect that negatively alters how we view prosperity, empire building, lifestyle choices, and our own priorities in life and church. In regards to reaching millennials and beyond, the evangelical church in North America is really struggling. There is a huge disconnect because young people are distancing themselves from the past baggage of the last several decades that haunt the contemporary church. Some of this is the fault of the millennial generation and some of it has to do with some unbiblical practices and teachings prevalent in many churches since the 1970s.

Since I preach in a lot of different places and have been involved in evangelism and overseeing a local church for several decades, I have often found it is not the Gospel that turns people off, but the people who are carrying the Gospel! I strongly urge church leadership to remove as many unnecessary stumbling blocks as possible so that as many people as possible will receive Christ.

The following points of evangelical disconnect with young people are based on conversations I have had with millennial leaders as well as with the average person on the street. Many of these maladies are the result of disconnecting the Gospel from the Kingdom, which leads to self-focus and narcissism.

An overemphasis on money

I have been in some services where the offering took more than thirty minutes—and this was the norm! In other services it was common to collect three or more offerings! Such practices give new people the impression that the church leadership is more concerned with collecting money than in preaching the Gospel, not to mention leaving the church open to suspicion regarding their motives. I believe money management and stewardship should be taught regularly, and at times, fundraising should be a focal point for in church gatherings, but none of these should ever consistently rival the time given to preaching and teaching the Word of God.

The opulent lifestyle of church leaders

In many cases, the lavish lifestyle of the lead pastor and other top leaders is a huge stumbling block for the Gospel. I believe God wants His children blessed, but the pastor and leaders should model a lifestyle of simplicity and not extravagance, especially if they lead churches in poor communities. The apostles Peter and Paul both stated that greed should not be a trait of church elders (see 1 Pet. 5:2; 1 Tim. 3:3).

Scandals

In this day and age, any fool can post something scandalous on social media about a church or leader that has no basis in the truth. This is a reality we cannot always avoid; hence, we should be slow to believe what people post about others! However, when leaders don't have proper boundaries in their finances and their personal life, they tend to cross the line in both. These are the ones who are ripe for a public scandal. From the huge televangelist scandals of the 1980s to the present, scandals in the church have given unbelievers another excuse not to repent and believe the Gospel. Every leader should be careful what they text, email, post, and say in public and in private. They should also have a strong interior life, in which they walk in the fear of the Lord, which enables all of us to depart from evil (see Prov. 16:6).

Duplicitous behavior

When children of believers and/or the unsaved witness ungodly behavior from their co-workers, employees, neighbors, and friends who claim to be Christians, it is a huge stumbling block to the Gospel. As Christians, we need to be people of our word and keep our promises, even if it hurts or costs us to do so.

Religious titles

Many millennials in certain communities are turned off by the excessive use of elaborate religious hierarchical titles. In some religious settings, everyone has a title like apostle, bishop apostle, Doctor, Reverend, or Archbishop. Young people are especially turned off by leaders who seem to need this kind of identification for self-validation.

Religious language

People in this generation are not as religious as the previous generation and feel disconnected when believers constantly use religious language in everyday communication. We have to learn to communicate using the "language of Babylon" if we hope to make strong connections with this generation. We have to teach believers how to "think biblically but speak secularly" if the Gospel is going to make inroads in our culture.

Religious images of power

Extravagant symbols of authority and power in the church turn off many young people. They more easily relate to down-to-earth, transparent leadership. When they see thrones on a church stage in which leaders are elevated above the congregation with pastors preaching (down) at the congregation, they get the wrong impression of leadership and are quickly disillusioned.

Religious behavior

Sometimes in church people have so many protocols, traditions, and rituals that they scare new people into thinking they have to become religious robots in order to believe. We need to show the world the difference between being religious (which does not save or sanctify a person) and having a relationship with the Lord Jesus. Young people today are looking for a genuine humanity coupled with a spirituality that is practical and powerful.

Empire building over Kingdom focus

Many people are turned off to the Gospel when they see leadership focused merely on their own agenda and building programs rather than serving the good of their community. God called us to serve our communities, not just build larger church buildings. They are distinctly not attracted to local church leadership who are all about building their own legacy and are interested only in ministry that emanates from their own church. They are likewise put off when a pastor or church are committed only to the things their local church does and not to citywide or national Christian outreach. Young people in particular are turned off when the entire focus is on Sunday ministry with no attention given to empowering people for their calling in the marketplace.

Programs over people

Many young people close their ears to the Gospel when they see the church focus more on events and programs than on relating one-on-one to people.

Triumphalism

Another off-putter for many young people are triumphalist prayers and pronouncements about taking cities and nations back for God. They feel called to serve their community but not to take it over by force. We in the church have to be careful with the kind of language we use to communicate our vision. The church is never called to "take a city," but to reach it by loving and serving it.

No community and authenticity

What young people crave most is community. Everyone needs to feel loved and to belong to an entity greater than himself or herself. Part of the call of the church is to assimilate new believers into the visible Body of Christ through relationships and discipleship. When people come to the church and experience only program-based Christianity, they will leave eventually and look for a real community in which to belong.

The personality-driven church

Finally, millennials are turned off when a church's marketing focus is mostly about the lead pastor rather than the church. Nothing leaves them colder than a local church website that is all about the ministry of the pastor—his profile, preaching, and great accomplishments—with little or no commensurate focus on what the church congregation is doing. Young people crave community and often have little patience with larger-than-life Christian personalities who dominate the local church scene.

When we combine the Gospel with the Kingdom, we neutralize the erroneous separation between clergy and the laity and empower all believers as ministers of God, instead of depending upon the so-called superstar lead pastor.

The Hebraic mindset of the Kingdom tends to emphasize the corporate community and its ability to permeate and transform culture rather than magnifying individual accomplishment and status.

Chapter Seven

The church failed to see how God intends marriage and family to be the key to cultural transformation.

> *"So God created man in his own image, in the image of God he created him; male and female he created them. And God blessed them. And God said to them, 'Be fruitful and multiply and fill the earth and subdue it and have dominion over the fish of the sea and over the birds of the heavens and over every living thing that moves on the earth'" (Genesis 1:27-28).*

When we separate the Gospel from the Kingdom we are left with marriage and family conceptually disconnected from the Cultural Mandate of Genesis 1:28. This strips from marriage any sense of Kingdom purpose except to win our children to God so they can go to heaven and have a nice family—and then repeat the same cycle. Unfortunately, many of our children will lose interest with this kind of Gospel if they feel it doesn't connect them to their earthly call to make a positive impact on the world. Once we embrace the Kingdom we will understand that God's plans and purposes are unpacked over multiple generations through God-fearing children who are trained to serve God by their parents and faith community (see Deut. 6:6-9).

Genesis 1:28 teaches us that having children (being fruitful) should ultimately result in believers filling the earth, subduing it, and having dominion over the created order! In order to understand this chapter, a brief exposition of Genesis 1:26-28 is necessary.

> *'Then God said, 'Let Us make man in Our image, according to Our likeness; let them have dominion over the fish of the sea, over the birds of the air, and over the cattle, over all the earth*

and over every creeping thing that creeps on the earth.' So God created man in His own image; in the image of God He created him; male and female He created them. Then God blessed them, and God said to them, 'Be fruitful and multiply; fill the earth and subdue it; have dominion over the fish of the sea, over the birds of the air, and over every living thing that moves on the earth'" (Genesis 1:26-28 NKJV).

As I have said numerous times, I believe Genesis 1:26-28 is the most important passage in the Bible regarding our purpose because it is the original covenant God made with man. Hence, it shows God's intent in making humans. When God the Father, Son, and Holy Spirit created humankind it took both male and female to accurately reflect who God is. Many people miss this point, mainly because God is referred to as Father. Scripture shows that God has a feminine, mothering nature as well as masculine qualities, but chose to be known as Father for some reason (probably because He identifies with more masculine than feminine qualities). It is vital that the church understand the roles of both males and females in revealing God's essence and nature. In fact, God's purpose and destiny for humanity cannot be fulfilled without both men and women working together.

This is best illustrated with the sacred institution of marriage, the first of six principles found in Genesis that show us how to bring God's dominion throughout the earth. As we read this passage we will notice that there are essentially six steps to Biblical Dominion. First, we see that both male and female are needed to reflect God's image (see Gen. 1:27). Because both men and women are made in the image of God it takes both working together to release the maximum blessing in any given sphere on the earth. Since God is a creative leader, women can also be in positions where their creativity flourishes in leadership capacity. Henceforth, women can function in most roles their male counterparts can, with few exceptions. (See Prov. 31:10-31 to discover how God has called both males and females to function in leadership roles in the world.)

Although both male and female are called to lead under God, there are vast differences between the two when functioning relationally in the context of the family, church, and marketplace. We are called to appreciate these biological and psychological differences and view them as complementary gifts to one another to fulfill the dominion mandate found in Genesis 1:28. The most important way to maximize the male/female reflection of God is through the holy institution of marriage in which the two become "one flesh" (Gen. 2:24). Becoming "one flesh" is the greatest concentration and example of reflecting the image of God possible in the world. In no other arrangement are people brought together as one flesh; hence, marriage between one man and one woman is the greatest example of reflecting and releasing God's image in the earth!

In these six steps to biblical dominion, **marriage is the first and foundational step** for all other steps to see God's rule released in our world. Strong and stable societies and churches are built upon strong marriages and families. This is why Satan loves divorce and cohabitation; both of these lifestyle choices water down this holy institution of marriage. Those living together without the commitment of marriage have a much higher divorce rate after they get married than those who wait until they are married to live together. Also, those abstaining from pre-marital sex have a much lower divorce rate than those engaging in sexual relations before marriage.

Furthermore, two-parent homes produce the healthiest children in regards to health, prosperity, and emotional well-being. Single moms have a very difficult time replacing a man in their child's life; both girls and boys need an involved father. A mother cannot function as both a mom and a dad (and neither can a father). When single moms receive the support from the men and women in their church it is much easier, but still not the same as a two-parent household. This is perhaps the greatest challenge facing our nation and the world today. American jails and prisons are filled with multiplied thousands of fatherless boys who grew up aimless because they lacked the two-parent expression of God's image in their childhood years.

The second step is to bear fruit (Genesis 1:28).

The primary meaning of Genesis 1:28 is to have children. Consequently, believing parents should shun abortion and stop planning for small families. (Of course, all people should work to end abortions.) We should pray over Genesis 1:28 and listen for God's voice when deciding how many children to have. Most women who get their tubes tied regret it later on. Also, the Muslims believe in Genesis 1:28 more than the church does. Consequently, they are gradually taking over all of Europe because the death rate among western Europeans is higher than the birth rate (about 1.5 children per family). For this reason, some European leaders believe their nations must import many immigrants, especially from Muslim nations in North Africa, to keep their economies afloat. I believe the greatest call of believers is to produce biological and spiritual children. Having biological children keeps the human race alive, while having spiritual children keeps the church alive and focused on its primary mission to win multitudes for Christ.

Multiply (Genesis 1:28)

God gave this command to Adam and Eve before they even had one child. From the very beginning, God was teaching them to have a generational mindset. Our children should have their own children. The greatest responsibility a parent has is to prepare their own children to be responsible individuals who can then reproduce their own stable families. God has called all of His people to think at least three generations ahead in everything they do. (See Psalm 78:5-8 in which God tells us to have regard for at least three generations, and Exodus 3:15 in which God identifies Himself to Moses as the God of Abraham, Isaac and Jacob–three generations.) This is another reason why all of us should faithfully tithe and give offerings to God, since we release a multi-generational blessing on our posterity. For the same reason we should use the blessings of God to get out of debt and have a plan to leave our children both a spiritual and family inheritance they can build upon.

Replenish the earth (Genesis 1:28)

One of the Hebrew root words for replenish means to consecrate, to make holy; hence, we are called to have children with the intent that they will fill the earth and commit it back to God. Thus, by implication, we are not only to have children but also keep our children in the faith and train them to be the leaders that will bring the earth realm back to God.

Every parent should take a few minutes every day praying and teaching the Bible to their young children; at least once per week they should have a family altar in which there is more serious discipleship of their children.

It is not the primary responsibility of the church to disciple children; the church can only aid parents. The church only has your child once or twice per week for a few hours; you have them 80 plus hours per week! The most important thing we do to train our children in the faith is to get them to serve in ministry as soon as possible, and for parents to live a consistent Christian life in the home. Even without a revival, if all the Christian families stopped aborting their children and worked to keep their children in the faith, we would have enough to out-vote all our opponents in general elections!

Subdue the Earth (Genesis 1:28)

Subdue means "to put under our feet." It thus implies taking power away from our enemies. When the church produces healthier families than the world, the result is more responsible children who will in turn take back the most important leadership positions from ungodly leaders. Thus, the godly will displace the ungodly as the gatekeepers of every cultural mountain. In the context of the church, however, we are not talking about subduing people by force but producing problem solvers and leaders in the world who will align systems of culture to its divine design.

Dominion (Genesis 1:28)

The end result of marriage and family is to manage the earth for God. We are called to train our children to be the leaders in the earth. Believers should not just teach their children to have a good job and move up in the company, but prepare them to start their own companies, their own banks, etc. Deuteronomy 28:13-14 says we are the head and not the tail; we are above and not beneath! God is calling the church to lead by serving our neighbors and being a blessing to the earth!

A church should be known throughout the community as a blessing. It should lift the economy, education, civic leadership, and the real estate of a whole community. If a church closes down and the community doesn't miss it, then it wasn't a real church anyway, just a spiritual social club! The church is not just called to save individual sinners but to replace ungodly systems with godly systems in politics, economics, education, social issues, health, the arts, science, etc. The church is called to disciple the nations. Read Matthew 28:18-20. (For more information on the topic of this chapter, I recommend my book *Walk in Generational Blessings*.[3]

---

3 Joseph Mattera, *Walk in Generational Blessings: Leaving a Legacy of Transformation through Your Family*. (Shippensburg, PA: Destiny Image Publishers, Inc., 2012).

Chapter Eight

The church fell into a dualism that separates Jesus as Redeemer from Jesus as Creator.

"All things were made through him, and without him was not anything made that was made" (John 1:3).

When we separated the Gospel from the Kingdom in the 19th century we largely stopped founding Christian universities (like Harvard, Yale, and Princeton that produced future leaders of nations in every aspect of life) and reduced our view of education to starting Bible institutes where young people learned the Bible apart from the human sciences and natural law. These institutes adapted to the semi-gnostic dualism of the church that taught that only spiritual things were important to God; thus, the physical world was unimportant! Gnosticism is a heretical view that arose during New Testament times and teaches that the material world was created and ruled by a lesser divinity known as a demi-urge, in contrast to Christ who was an emissary of the Supreme Being, whose focus is on the spiritual world and the human spirit.

This dualistic hyper-dispensational theology became popular after the Civil War and, as I said before, led to the church abandoning culture and leaving the stewardship of the nation to the secular humanists. As a result, the church lost the culture in just one generation. Truly, any sphere that the church refuses to influence will come back and attempt to destroy her! When we fall into separating the natural from the spiritual world and make the latter more important than the former, we separate Jesus as Redeemer from Jesus as Creator! The Jesus who saves us in John 1:12 is the same Jesus who, according to John 1:3, created the systems of the universe.

When we connect the Gospel to the Kingdom we find that we are compelled by the Spirit of God to participate in all things related to creation care, such as politics, economics, education, law, policy, the environment, nutrition, and all the natural sciences, as well as depicting natural beauty through music, the arts, literature, and entertainment. Unfortunately, by the late 1880s the much of the American church had jettisoned the Kingdom message and adopted a hyper-dispensational view of Scripture that moved the church away from stewarding the natural world to focusing almost exclusively on things spiritual. One significant consequence of this theological turn was an obsessive interest in "the last days" and the "rapture," which some regard as "semi-gnostic" because many of those so obsessed with escaping the earth lose interest in the practical matters of stewarding the earth. Because they are convinced that the world soon will be taken over by the "Antichrist," they consider efforts to reform society to be as useless as re-arranging deck chairs on the Titanic.

However, dispensational theology is less than two hundred years old and has not been the historic eschatological position of the church. Eschatology is very important, since your eschatology (view of the last days) determines your protology (your view of first things, origins, and God's purpose for humanity). Chances are, if your eschatology emphasizes that the last days are here now, you will find it harder (and theologically inconsistent) to become motivated to apply your faith to engaging contemporary culture. There are several eschatological positions that can lead a person to a semi-gnostic view of faith and the world.

Throughout Christian history, various eschatological views have emerged that have led many believers and churches to non-engagement with surrounding cultures in favor of escapism. Generally these positions have been similar in essence to Gnosticism and Platonism (from the Greek philosopher Plato). In these views, the natural world is considered unimportant or evil, resulting in an almost exclusive emphasis on the spiritual ideal and the next life. Since my intention in this chapter is to show the cultural implications of these views, I will make no attempt to provide theological explanations for each position. Many fine books are available for that purpose.

Following are three prominent eschatological views that potentially can lead to a semi-gnostic view of Christianity.

Hyper-Premillennial Dispensational Eschatology

This is the view systemized by J.N. Darby in the late 19th century, made popular with the Scofield and Dakes Bibles in the 20th century and by many other books by authors such as Hal Lindsey and Tim LaHaye during the 1970s-1990s. According to this view, believers in Jesus will soon be caught up with the Lord in heaven (the rapture) before or in the middle of a future seven-year Great Tribulation, during which time the Satan-possessed Antichrist rules over the territories of the ancient Roman Empire. This cataclysmic event results in thousands of Jews being saved (144,000 as per their interpretation of the book of Revelation), the turning of Israel to Christ, and the inauguration of a great global revival that will culminate with the bodily return of Jesus Christ to judge the nations and usher in a thousand-year millennial reign.

Without getting into details, this relatively new view (the rapture wasn't widely taught until the mid-1800s) has been rejected by an overwhelming majority of Evangelical scholars over the past 20 years. Basically, this view of the end times overrides numerous New Testament interpretations of Old Testament promises regarding Israel, arriving at an Israel-centric position in which the church is merely a parenthetical people in a holding pattern (based on a particular interpretation of Daniel 9:24-27), awaiting the rapture until the remnant of chosen biological Jews (the 144,000 of Revelation 7) get their act together by receiving Christ.

The logical result of this post-Civil War eschatological position has been the church's virtual abandonment of culture to secular humanism. Adherents of this view believe that it will be primarily the converted Jews who will bring about world revival; that the Antichrist is going to take over everything anyway; and that the nations will not be Christianized until the return of the Lord Jesus Christ. Why, they reason, waste time and energy rearranging deck chairs on the Titanic? Why try to convert a culture that will not be converted until after Christ returns anyway?

Although some notable leaders with this eschatological position, such as Jerry Falwell, Pat Robertson, Tim LaHaye, and others, have attempted to reform America, one cannot deny the facts of recent church history illustrating that the American church as a whole generally lost its reformation zeal after the Civil War, when it moved from a post-millennial Puritan eschatological view to a hyper-premillennial view. Leaders with this position generally have to go against their eschatological view of looming apostasy, defeat, and escape for the present-day church in order to work towards their goals of political and cultural transformation.

In my opinion, this is inconsistent at best and schizophrenic at worst! The truth is, most believers with this view are not engaged socially. They "check out" of this world, don't believe in a victorious future church, and pray for the second coming of Christ when things get rough! I know: I was one of them for my first 17 years as a Christian!

Hyper-Preterism

Hyper-preterism, or full preterism, is the opposite extreme of the view above. It teaches that the Book of Revelation and all New Testament prophecies have already been fulfilled with the destruction of the Jewish temple in A.D. 70. These fulfilled prophecies include the second coming of Christ, the resurrection of the dead, the coming of Antichrist, etc. Like the hyper-premillennial dispensational view above, this view is a late theological development with no major theologians holding to it until the 1900s. Although I agree with some form of preterism (for example, many of the prophecies of Matthew 24 and the Book of Revelation were fulfilled with the destruction of the temple in A.D. 70), I still have several significant problems with this view.

If the resurrection of all believers is merely spiritual and not physical, then what about the teaching in Acts 1 in which the angels say that in the same manner Christ ascended into heaven He will return? His resurrection and ascension include a physical body (see Lk. 24:39; Jn. 20:27; Acts 1:9-11), not only a spiritual body. Thus, this view comports with the Gnostic theme of spiritualizing everything and disregarding Christ's humanity and the material world! Since Adam's sin had physical effects (for example, bodily death and disease) and not just spiritual effects, this view also denies the physical reality of our walk with God. First Corinthians 6:19 teaches that our physical bodies are temples of the Holy Spirit. Thus, if believers are presently fulfilling the full resurrection experience of the New Testament, then the physical world has been deemphasized by Scripture and the Gnostic Christians which John the apostle warned against were in some ways correct (1 John 4:2).

Furthermore, if all biblical prophecies have already been fulfilled, then the cultural commission of Matthew 28:18-20 is no longer in force. Jesus said in that passage that He would be with His disciples to the end of the age, which consistent hyper-preterists must interpret as being fulfilled in the generation between the resurrection and the destruction of the temple in A.D. 70. Colossians 1:5-6 is the passage they cite to prove this. Thus, no longer would there be an impetus to reform the nations for Christ; the future could continue with sin dwelling on the earth ad infinitum. Such a view could lead us into the error of spiritualizing our present Christian journey into a sort of Gnostic existentialism and mysticism, rather than producing cultural reform.

Finally, all the historic creeds of the church (Apostles' Creed, Nicene Creed, etc.) teach that there will be a literal, bodily second coming of Christ and the bodily resurrection of all the saints. Any view that disregards the hermeneutical grid of the early church bypasses the human process God uses to teach the collective church through the Holy Spirit, thus elevating a mystical, individualistic hermeneutical illumination of the Bible that coincides with early Gnosticism.

Amillennialism

Throughout history the majority of the church, generally speaking, has been postmillennial in viewpoint. That is, the church has believed that Christ is presently reigning in heaven with the saints in glory and through the church on earth, and will return physically after the millennial reign. (The "1000 years" is only mentioned six times in the Book of Revelation, which is a highly symbolic book. For example, the 1,000 years mentioned in Revelation 20 historically has been interpreted by many theologians to refer to a long but indefinite period of time, not literally 1,000 years.)

With the advent of many eschatological views in the past 200 years a new term, amillennialism, was introduced as an alternative and contrast to post-millennialism. The major difference between these two concepts lies in their understanding of the nature of Christ's millennial reign. Post-millennialists believe that Christ's reign will be physically and spiritually manifested on earth through the church fulfilling the cultural commission of Genesis 1:28 and Matthew 28:19-20, putting God's enemies under His feet before Jesus returns bodily to judge the world. (This interpretation is based on Ps. 110:1-2 and Acts 3:21, among other passages). Amillennialists, for their part, believe that Jesus is already reigning spiritually in heaven with the saints who have passed into glory. Because His kingdom is not of this world (see Jn. 18:36), this view does not depend on a political or social reformation for Him to return bodily.

The problem with amillennialism is its failure to integrate the cultural commission as an essential component of eschatology, considered unnecessary, in their view, due to the spiritual nature of Jesus' reign. Thus, amillennialists cannot fully account for prominent passages such as Genesis 1:28, Psalm 2, Psalm 110:1-2, Acts 3:21, Revelation 3:26, and others that covenantally connect both testaments.

Consequently, a person who believes the reign of Christ is merely spiritual and not earthly knows not what to do with the Lord's Prayer, specifically Jesus' teaching to ask God for His Kingdom to come and His will to be done ON EARTH as it is in heaven. In addition, since Jesus' reign is spiritual and will never be manifest on earth through the church, one could hold to any political, economic, or policy view, and even be a total liberal where morality is concerned, and it would not matter. Like hyper-premillennialism, the amillennial church is in some sort of neutral holding pattern concerned only with spiritual things until the return of our Lord Jesus Christ! Obviously, this view could also cause believers to fall into a sort of Gnosticism if they do not attempt to seriously incorporate the cultural commission into their theological position.

Postmillennialism

Post-millennialists are also divergent in their views. Some expect a future thousand-year golden age for the church before Christ returns. Others, like myself, believe, like amillennialists, that the reign of Christ is not literally a physical 1,000-year future period. I believe this because Scripture teaches that the church (in heaven and on earth) has been reigning with Christ since the inauguration of the Kingdom (see Mk. 1:15; Rom. 5:17; and Eph. 1:17-2:26). Post-millennialists allow for both a spiritual reign in heaven and a gradual manifestation of Christ's Kingdom on the earth before His return. They believe that the biblical covenants (starting with Genesis 1:28) are still in force on the earth and are revealed by the blessings and curses God bestows on individuals and nations commensurate to the degree to which they accept or reject the laws of God and the Gospel of Christ.

Lest anyone attempt to criticize me for adhering to some new-fangled eschatology, I want to make sure you understand that the majority of the early church and Reformation theologians held to some form of post-millennialism, although it took centuries to unpack Scripture and systematize it. Its adherents stand in the tradition of august historians and theologians such as Eusebius (A.D. 260-340), Athanasius (A.D. 296-372), Augustine (A.D. 354-430), Jonathan Edwards (1703-1758), William Carey (1761-1834), Charles Hodge (1797-1878), James Henley Thornwell (1812-1862), Robert Dabney (1820-1898), William G.T. Shedd (1820-1894), Augustus Strong (1836-1921), H.C.G. Moule (1841-1920), B.B. Warfield (1851-1921), J. Gresham Machen (1881-1937), John Murray (1898-1975), Loraine Boettner (1903-1989), and Greg Bahnsen (1948-1995) to name a few, plus many other contemporary theologians too numerous to cite here.

In spite of all of our serious differences, there have been many great people of God who have impacted the world who stand in each of these camps. Also, notable adherents of each of the major millennial systems all agree that the full manifestation of the Kingdom of God will never come until the bodily return of Christ (although, as stated before, hyper-preterists believe the final return of Christ already took place!)

For further study on these positions, I recommend:

The Incredible Scofield and His Book, by Joseph M. Canfield, a powerful critique of hyper-dispensational theology.

Hal Lindsey and the Restoration of the Jews, by Steve Schlissel and David Brown, a powerful correction to the dispensational teaching of Hal Lindsey regarding Israel's future.

The Rapture Plot, by Dave MacPherson, a book that uncovers the suspect history of how the rapture became a major belief in the church; it also shows that prior to 1830 no such teaching ever existed throughout church history!

Matthew 24 Fulfilled, by John L. Bray, shows the partial preterist view of many last days prophecies.

A Case for Amillennialism, by Kim Riddlebarger, a great book showing the classical amillennial view.

Paradise Restored, and *The Days of Vengeance,* by David Chilton, classic books showing the post-millennial, partial-preterist view of Scripture.

He Shall Have Dominion, by Kenneth Gentry, an easy read on the major millennial views and their historical precedents. A must read for those wanting to understand the post-millennial position.

Revelation: Four Views: A Parallel Commentary, edited by Steve Gregg, a great book presenting four parallel views of the last days.

In conclusion, when we connect the Gospel to the Kingdom, we will not only place importance on things spiritual (prayer, healing, deliverance, and evangelism) but also on the created order and things natural (natural law, the environment, and all things regarding creation care).

Chapter Nine

The church limited its ability to impact principalities over nations who rule through ideologies.

> *"For the weapons of our warfare are not carnal but mighty through God for pulling down strongholds, casting down arguments and every high thing that exalts itself against the knowledge of God, bringing every thought in captivity to the obedience of Christ" (2 Corinthians 10:4-5 NKJV).*

According to 2 Corinthians 10:4-5, the strongholds in the world we struggle against are based on thoughts and imaginations. When we start dealing with the Kingdom of God, we are dealing with worldview issues, the very stuff that principalities over nations use to rule over humanity. When we preach an individual gospel, we deal merely with demons oppressing individual people. When we deal with the Kingdom, we confront principalities who work through systems of economics, education, policy, and politics! Principalities work primarily through humanistic ideologies and philosophies that become the worldview of a nation or culture. Kingdom focus enables us to pray fully the Lord's Prayer (Lk. 11:2-4), in which Jesus teaches the church to pray for His kingdom to come and His will to be done on earth as it is in heaven. This releases intercessors to go to a higher level of authority and focus, which will lead to systemic change. Demons deal with individual sinners; principalities (as seen in Daniel chapters 10,12) deal with nations and systems.

Ephesians 3:10 teaches us that the principalities or rulers (invisible archetypes who influence the visible world of humans) learn the wisdom of God through the church. The Greek word for wisdom in that verse is *sofia*, which has to do with the wisdom of God as demonstrated in His government and councils. Hence, if the church is dealing only with individual mystical issues, the demonic rulers will run rampant in our nation. However, if the church is revealing the wisdom of God to the ruling angelic hosts of heaven, we release them to manifest the reign of God on the earth in our communities and nations.

I remember the following personal snapshot like it was yesterday (about three years after I was illuminated regarding the Gospel of the Kingdom). On January 2, 1998, a strong spirit of prayer came upon me. The burden of God upon my heart was so heavy that I was barely able to speak to anyone. I had to alter my schedule since my heart was drawn out to God to push off this burden between three and eight hours per day. This heavy burden of prayer lasted for three years!

One day, after more than a year of living this way, I asked the Lord why this was happening. I sensed an impression that God was now taking me to another level of authority in ministry, a level where I would confront a higher level in the demonic realm. God was preparing me in the spirit so that when He took me out of hiding to preach on the Kingdom to the nations, I would be ready for the intense pressure and warfare I would face. (For more information on this kind of prayer, refer to my book, *Travail to Prevail*, available on Amazon.)

Consequently, I do not dare get up to preach without spending adequate time waiting upon God, being filled with His Spirit, and walking in His power and grace. Also, whenever I minister in a conference or conduct trans-local ministry, I send specific prayer requests to about forty high-level intercessors who are committed to intercede for me and my family. Bringing about true and lasting change to a local church, community, or nation calls for protracted and intense intercession and travail so that the purposes of God can be birthed. If all we do is preach nice messages we will merely engage the minds, and not the hearts of the hearers.

The bottom line is that we each need to ask ourselves, "Am I seeking God commensurate to the calling on my life"? If we rarely spend time with God, it may be because we think we don't have a high calling from God. Otherwise, we would be living a life of dependence upon Him. The things God has called us to do should be so challenging that only God can accomplish the work. Our part is to be willing human vessels that give Him space to operate in and through us.

A case in point: the prophet Daniel regularly prayed and fasted because he was always involved in shifting whole nations and empires. Reading through the book of Daniel (especially chapters 10-12), we find that he regularly prayed for the restoration of his nation, Israel, and witnessed firsthand the activity of principalities who had influence over the empires of Babylon, Persia, and Greece. Due to his intense walk with God he never compromised his faith even though he was surrounded by pagan priests and practitioners of the magic arts (see Dan. 1:20).

Consequently, those of us who preach and practice the things concerning the Kingdom of God are required to have a robust prayer life and passion for God if we hope to be effective. This is for two reasons: first, mere theology, preaching, and training people in the biblical worldview is very important, but not enough to prepare them to be world changing disciples of Christ. Theology can merely appeal to the intellect of the disciple, which doesn't necessarily translate into having enough power to bring results (see 1 Cor. 2:1-4). Second, a person who proclaims the Kingdom of God without the anointing of the Holy Spirit will lack the power needed to change the hearts and lives of people. Only those with a strong, passionate walk with God can represent His Kingdom adequately enough to see people totally transformed.

My prayer as I conclude this chapter is that those of us who preach the Gospel of the Kingdom not only prepare ourselves with rigorous biblical studies, but also by endeavoring to seek Him commensurate to our divine assignment. May we also combine the Gospel with the Kingdom so we can affect principalities over nations and not just individual demons who oppress individual people.

Chapter Ten

The church attracted fewer men.

"And more than ever believers were added to the Lord, multitudes of both men and women" (Acts 5:14).

If we separate the Gospel from the Kingdom we remove motivation from the majority of men who will never feel called to full-time church work. Adam was tilling the Garden of Eden even before he was married (see Gen. 2), which means that men have an innate desire to work and exercise dominion over the created order that precedes the formation of their family! Of course, having a wife and children should give a man balance and better focus, but you cannot separate a man from his desire to work and having dominion on the earth. Consequently, when the church focuses on escaping the earth rather than tilling it and stewarding it, they lull many men to sleep because men naturally search for meaning and truth through their work, not apart from it. I believe that if we connect the Gospel to the Kingdom, our churches will be teeming with men!

This will be most welcome to many churches that have an average male attendance of 25% or less. Perhaps the biggest need I have seen in the Body of Christ since entering full-time ministry in 1980 is the lack of male church attendance. This is especially true in Charismatic/Pentecostal churches in North America. In many churches, male attendance comprises only 15% of the Sunday gender demographic. There are some exceptions to this: in our local church, male attendance is typically 35-40%, and Christian Cultural Center in Brooklyn, New York, has had a male church attendance of about 51%.

In many cases men are dragged to church every Sunday by either their girlfriends or wives. This is a serious issue because statistics have shown that when a father attends church regularly, there is an 85% probability that his spouse and children will attend as well. Contrariwise, when only the wife attends church, her family will follow only 15% of the time. My observations of my own local church also bear this out.

I have spent much time pondering this issue. The following are some reasons why I believe this has occurred:

- Many churches do not clearly articulate their vision. Men are generally task-oriented and are motivated by vision and purpose.
- Sunday messages are often more hype than practical teaching with substance. Men are often very cognitive and logical, and crave practical teaching that will equip them to be better fathers, husbands, and businessmen.
- Sunday worship often involves excessive displays of emotion that make men feel uncomfortable.
- Sunday worship is often 45 minutes or longer, which is way too long for the average first-time male visitor.
- Sunday services are too long, with lengthy announcements and other elongated verbiage most men deem unnecessary.
- There is a lack of male leadership among the pastors, elders, deacons, and ministry team. The situation is even more exacerbated in cases when the senior pastor is a female, although this is improving in the corporate world. Most strong men have a hard time submitting to a female executive leader in a church setting. I am told there are some rare exceptions to this, although I have never witnessed one firsthand.
- There is often a lack of male bonding, fellowship, and men's discipleship in congregations. While most churches have many socials and activities for the women, many churches lack the same focus on men's activities and events.

- Men in marketplace leadership are not affirmed. Many businessmen feel their leadership gifting is not recognized in the local church; they are viewed only as cash cows to fund the local church.
- The feminization of Christianity has caused numerous men to see Jesus and Christianity as wimpy and effeminate. The Anabaptist concept of pacifism has infiltrated the Evangelical world and emasculated men's innate desires to both defend and protect their families and country. For example, "turning the other cheek" in Matthew 5 has been misunderstood to mean a man cannot go to war for his country and defend his family when they are threatened with bodily harm. This cannot be what Jesus meant, since going to war was expected in the Old Testament. Romans 13:4-7 teaches that magistrates act as God's ministers when they use the sword to protect their citizens, and Jesus Himself resisted evil forcibly when He drove the money changers and thieves out of the temple. Thus, we conclude that "turning the other cheek" means Christians should not fight merely if they are insulted, since being slapped on the cheek represents no mortal threat, but is only a way of insulting the victim.
- Many churches emphasize a feelings-centered subjective relationship with God rather than objective principle-centered faith based on the Word of God. Many men are uncomfortable expressing their inner feelings in public. Although feelings are important, it should also be emphasized that faith is first, then correct feelings will follow.
- Many churches celebrate Mother's Day but ignore Father's Day, due to family fragmentation and divorce. Often, boys are brought up by single mothers and do not even know how to relate to their earthly fathers and other male authority figures.

- Many of the words in contemporary songs emphasize the church as the bride of Christ, thus emphasizing the believer's role as the receiver in the relationship (a feminine position much like the wife in a marriage) instead of balancing out the songs with hymns and lyrics that emphasize Christ as King and His church as His army called forth to conquer the nations for Him. Another way of saying it is that worship is often "bedroom" rather than "throne room" in its essence. That is to say, much of the worship is feminine in nature with expressions of passion, love, and intimacy for Jesus that make many men uncomfortable. Throne room worship emphasizes the Lordship and Kingship of Christ, which is more easily relatable to male church attendees. I am not saying here that we should do away with "bedroom" worship, but that we should also equally connect to God with "throne room" worship for a proper balance in congregational assemblies.
- In many urban communities, many boys are raised in fragmented families by single mothers, thus making it harder to disciple them when they come into the church. Generally, a woman does not have the capability to balance nurturing with strong correction to properly raise up a boy to manhood. Thus, boys often are undisciplined and not used to the confines of structure and male authority. The exception is when a boy is either in the military or team sports, in which the male coach becomes a surrogate father exerting authority in the boy's life.
- Many men (businessmen in particular) will attach themselves to a successful enterprise exhibiting a spirit of excellence and fiscal responsibility. This is a far cry from many shabby church operations, in which the pastor runs a mom-and-pop shop with autocratic control without fiscal disclosure, accountability, and proper church government.

Recommended books to read on this subject include: *Missing from Action: A Powerful Historical Response to the Crisis among American Men*, by Weldon Hardenbrook and Terry Somerville[4]

The Church Impotent: The Feminization of Christianity, by Leon J. Podles[5]

---

4 Weldon M. Hardenbrook with Terry Somerville, *Missing from Action: A Powerful Historical Response to the Crisis among American Men*. (Ben Lomond, CA: Conciliar Press, 1996).

5 Leon J. Podles, *The Church Impotent: The Feminization of Christianity*. (Dallas, TX: Spence Publishing Co., 1999).

Chapter Eleven

The church misinterpreted key passages in Scripture.

"Be diligent to present yourself approved to God as a workman who does not need to be ashamed, accurately handling the word of truth" (2 Timothy 2:15).

One of the greatest things that happened to me when I came to understand the Gospel of the Kingdom was that the Word of God was greatly enhanced in my understanding. It was like I put on "Kingdom glasses" that enabled me to see things in Scripture I had never seen before because of a faulty paradigm that limited my thinking. I found that I had a whole new Bible!

Unfortunately, my previous limited paradigm led me to misinterpret many key passages of Scripture. For example, before I came into the Kingdom message in 1995, I used to preach that unless a person is "born again" they will not go to heaven. However, after I was illuminated by God to understand the Kingdom, I re-read that passage in John 3:1-8 and saw that "seeing the Kingdom" had nothing to do with going to heaven; Jesus was referring to an experience of "seeing" or "experiencing" the Kingdom instantly upon the moment of conversion.

Basically, what Jesus was saying was that when He comes into a person's life, that person's spiritual eyes are opened to see and understand for the first time that Jesus is Lord of all. Included with this is the intuition that the earth and the whole universe are under the rule of God's Kingdom, both visible and invisible. Hence, being born again has nothing to do with going to a geographical location called heaven, but understanding that Jesus is reigning in the here and now, not just in the afterlife.

Another passage often misinterpreted is John 3:16, which is perhaps the most popular verse in the whole Bible! Before I came into the Kingdom message I thought this passage referred only to an individual person being saved from hell when He believed in the Lord Jesus. Although this is certainly true, the revelation of the Kingdom greatly enhances this passage. Now when I read this verse I look beneath the surface and investigate its full implications. For example, the word "world" in John 3:16 is the Greek word *kosmos*, which means not only the people who live in the world but also the systems that support civilization.

Also, the word "perish" in Greek is *appolomi*, which is the same Greek word used to describe the destruction of the old wineskin after new wine is poured into it (see Mk. 2:19-22). This wineskin did not go to hell and did not cease to exist anymore; it just could not fulfill its intended purpose. In light of the above, the expanded and implied meaning of John 3:16 is as follows:

God so loved the people and the systems of the world (politics, economics, education, music, art, science, law, ethics…) that He gave His only Son, that whoever believes in Him (obeys Him, aligns their life under Him) will not "perish" (will not waste their life and miss their divine assignment) but have eternal life (they will experience the power, the presence, and the freedom of Christ in the here and now so they can fulfill their assignment on the earth).

When I separated the Gospel from the Kingdom I had an individualistic theological paradigm that did not allow me to see anything more than the individual blessings of the Gospel. Now you can see why my "Kingdom conversion" granted me a new set of glasses so I could read a whole new expanded Bible! When you connect the Gospel to the Kingdom you do not do away with the individual salvation message; you just understand the vastness of it and how it is connected to the reign of Christ over all things in the creation.

(For more on this subject, check out my books *Ruling in the Gates*; *Understanding the Wineskin of the Kingdom*; and *25 Truths You Never Heard in Church*.[6]

6 Joseph Mattera, *Ruling in the Gates: Preparing the Church to Transform Cities*. (Lake Mary, FL: Creation House Press, a part of Strang Communications Company, 2003); Joseph Mattera, *Understanding the Wineskin of the Kingdom*. (Chambersburg, PA: eGenCo, 2016); Joseph Mattera, *25 Truths You Never Heard in Church: Becoming a Kingdom-Focused Believer*. (Chambersburg, PA: eGenCo, 2017).

Chapter Twelve

The church used Christianity as a means of escape rather than engaging the world.

"Thy kingdom come. Thy will be done in earth, as it is in heaven" (Luke 11:2 KJV).

When His disciples asked Jesus how to pray, He responded by giving them a way to focus their life properly, not just a template for prayer. After all, Jesus would never separate prayer from His overarching purpose for believers. Jesus' target in prayer always was for His Kingdom or His reign to come on the *earth*, not heaven.

Unfortunately, when we separate the Gospel from the Kingdom we are left without a proper focus on the earth, with the result that believers merely live for and anticipate the next life, to the neglect of their earthly call.

The Bible, in fact, says very little about heaven. God's Word is not a book about heaven nearly as much as it is about the earth. Specifically, the Bible is the most practical book ever written about how believers are called to steward the earth! Hence, the focus of the Scriptures and of Jesus was not about going to heaven but about how to represent God as His stewards on planet earth. Essentially, the Bible is a book about how to manage the planet.

In the late 1800s, the church's transition from preaching the Gospel of the Kingdom to preaching an individualistic gospel also brought about a transition from engaging the earth to escaping the earth. This disengagement was catastrophic, resulting in the church's loss of every institute of higher learning by the early 20th century and of the entire culture by the 1960s. Jesus called all believers to function as the salt of the earth and the light of the world (see Matt. 5:13-16), and when we fail to do this, people of other belief systems attempt to function as earthly luminaries. When the church separated the Gospel from the Kingdom, it lost its sense of obligation to serve its communities. We focused on preaching and teaching the "good news" to ourselves! The only thing we cared about was self-preservation and personal salvation. This is how the preponderance of believers lost any sense of personal responsibility to influence the culture; such a role was no longer connected to their faith.

Cultural disengagement caused the church to take a decidedly mystical turn, longing more for the rapture than for winning nations to Christ—despite the fact that Jesus commanded His followers to "Occupy till I come" (Lk. 19:13 KJV). The word occupy refers to taking territories and being responsible stewards. Consequently, anticipation of the second bodily return of Christ should motivate believers to engage culture, not retreat from it in expectation of escaping it completely. Maintaining the connection between the Gospel and the Kingdom gives us the impetus to labor for a Kingdom witness in all the world before Christ returns for His bride (see Matt. 24:14).

As a matter of fact, when we pray for the rapture (for many, Jesus coming to rescue the true church from the earth before His bodily return), we actually are praying *against* Jesus' own prayer to His Father in John 17:15: "My prayer is not that you take them (the church) out of the world but that you protect them from the evil one." In this "High-Priestly" prayer, Jesus actually was praying against the present day mindset of "rapture-focused" believers! His focus for the church is the earth, not heaven; it is for engagement, not escape; it is practical, not mystical.

Thus, when we connect the Gospel to the Kingdom, we properly align ourselves to the prayer focus of Jesus Himself, who wanted His people to manifest His Kingdom upon earth and did not want them to run from the conflicts of the world. Only when the church once again preaches the Gospel of the Kingdom will we have a theology big enough to serve cities and disciple whole nations.

Chapter Thirteen

The church built its own kingdom.

"Jesus answered, 'My kingdom is not of this world'" (John 18:36).

Ever since the Western and Eastern branches of Christianity divided in the eleventh century, some of the greatest fears of the once-united Christendom have been realized: fragmentation and division. Even in the sixteenth century, when Martin Luther and John Calvin led the Protestant Reformation, it was hoped there would only be a few major expressions of the Body of Christ. Never in their wildest imaginations did the Reformers envision the dizzying plethora of denominations, sects, and various other branches and networks of Christianity that have since evolved. This has given opportunity for a spirit of lawlessness, independence, and empire-building to arise among some gifted, yet insecure, leaders. Determining whether or not all these varied expressions are of God is not the purpose of this section of the book.

This issue is nothing new; human nature has been self-focused ever since man's fall in the Garden of Eden. Perhaps no biblical account epitomizes mankind's pride and hubris better than the ancient human race's attempt to build the "Tower of Babel," which led to God's judgement by scattering them throughout the whole earth (see Gen. 11:1-18). Similarly, in 1 Kings 11:11 and 12:16, God divided the kingdom of Israel because of religious apostasy. This is the same reason the Catholic Church was judged and fragmented; there was too much concentration of power in the hands of humans who deviated from the true ways of Jesus Christ and the apostles. God will judge His church and hold back revival from certain churches, ministries, and regions when their key spiritual leaders are focused on building their own empires rather than building the Kingdom of God. Leaders may talk the talk, but for many, their actions speak louder than their so-called "Kingdom-first" words.

Let us now consider 17 characteristics of Christian leaders who are empire builders rather than Kingdom builders.

1. Empire builders rejoice when other key leaders in your region are struggling.

Although all leaders say they are sad when another church, pastor, or leader in their area is struggling, I have observed that some leaders seem privately to gloat or compare themselves favorably against failing leaders in their area. Whether the failing church or leader is right or wrong, it never pleases God when we internally rejoice or gloat when the Body of Christ is not advancing in our region.

2. Empire builders are territorial and only work with those under their "covering."

Some leaders and denominations will only do outreaches with churches and leaders who have a ministerial and financial allegiance with them. If we are going to reach our communities we must be willing to cross denominations and networks and work with the leaders who are sincerely committed to advancing the Kingdom of God.

3. Empire builders only support events that give them a platform.

I have seen leaders actually pull out of a citywide or community event because their name was not advertised on the program or because a personal "rival" was part of the program. This reveals that their true concern is not advancing the Kingdom but advancing their own name and building their own empire.

4. Empire builders tend to exaggerate their own importance and influence to outsiders.

Empire builders treat their ministries like sporting events; they are constantly throwing around numbers and stats, and comparing their numbers to the numbers of other ministers. They say things like, "We are growing in record numbers" or, "This was the most significant event in our city" or, "We have the largest network in our city." Worse yet is when they claim that their ministry is the sole reason why God moves in their community or region.

Empire builders tend to exaggerate their influence, importance, and results in their region or community. I have observed that several so-called revivals in our country in recent years, rather than genuine moves of God, have been nothing more than good advertising and marketing. Conversely, Kingdom builders brag about what God is doing through His church in His city. They also attempt to applaud the success of others whose feet they wash instead of propping themselves up for photo shoots and publicity.

5. Empire builders are jealous of successful key leaders in their region.

I know I am with an empire builder when that person is always attempting to dig up dirt on other leaders, criticizing key leaders in the community, or giving faint praise when asked about other key leaders in the region.

6. Empire builders speak about Kingdom unity as a smokescreen to hide their own selfish agenda.

Some of the most self-centered empire builders I have known have spoken the most in public about the need for unity in the Body of Christ. They use this kind of talk to get sheep, pastors, and other ministers to forsake their own agendas and follow them to aid in building their empire!

They know all the lingo and have all the biblical passages down pat, but unfortunately their actions do not correspond with their words and preaching.

7. Empire builders' name and picture must be highlighted in every event in which they participate.

There are leaders I have heard speak about God raising up a movement of nameless and faceless people, yet in all their conferences, literature, and advertising, their picture and name are highlighted more prominently and more often than anyone or anything else in the program! I even attended one conference that featured a life-size picture of the leader in the lobby, with the event itself and all its program elements posted in small print under his picture!

8. Empire builders try to steal the loyalty of people connected to other ministries.

One of the key signs of an empire builder I have observed is when someone goes after key leaders in other leaders' churches or networks. As a personal example, a number of years ago, I learned that several leaders representing our Christ Covenant Coalition were approached by another leader in my city, who asked them to join his network as a representative, despite knowing that these leaders had been part of the CCC leadership for over ten years!

Whenever leaders do this kind of thing, they make themselves look bad, both to the loyal leaders they approach as well as other key leaders in the city once they learn of the *modus operandi* of these empire builders.

9. Empire builders love those who follow them and disregard all others.

Empire builders have an "either you are with me or against me" mentality and approach to life. They will not be friends with a person if that person is connected to the ministry of a rival. One of my regional leaders actually told me several years ago that he was no longer welcome to preach in a particular church because he was keeping the company of certain other leaders. Because empire builders are untrustworthy and use their pseudo-friendships as a platform to perpetuate their own empires, they project that same spirit and mentality on other leaders in their region. Thus, they cut off people loyal to other networks and ministries because they suspect in others the same untrustworthiness that they are blind to in themselves!

10. Empire builders have a top-down leadership approach and struggle to attract strong, successful leaders.

Empire builders surround themselves with "yes men" and actually discourage strong, resourceful leaders from working or partnering with them, since doing so does not fit their top-down leadership style. Unlike mature leaders who take a bottom-up approach in which they try to lead through consensus with multiple participation at various levels with people taking responsibility in ministry (so that all have ownership in the process), empire builders surround themselves with leaders of ministries they deem less significant who will follow their dictates without attempting meaningful, strategic dialogue.

11. Empire builders are self-driven rather than led by the Spirit.

Empire builders have an intense need for affirmation because their insecurity—not the glory of God and work of advancing the Kingdom—drives their need for success. Thus, they rarely know inner peace or rest because they are striving constantly to create a platform and expand their ministry by their own efforts instead of allowing the Lord to lead them and bring them opportunities and open doors.

12. Empire builders are opportunists when other ministries are struggling.

Empire builders pretend they are concerned when other churches or ministries are struggling, but then attempt to maneuver themselves so they can capitalize on the struggles of other ministries. They either seize their property or, more likely, their choicest leaders and key people.

13. Empire builders' main goal in life is to build some kind of monument to their success.

Empire builders are obsessed with building bigger and better buildings and acquiring more and more property, even if they have to take on huge debt to do it. The lower their self-esteem, the bigger they have to build to compensate for their internal lack. Unfortunately, they often risk the future of their ministries with excessive spending and rarely, if ever, think about how their successor is going to fill all these buildings and pay off the mortgage! Remember, there is never any real success without a successor!

14. Empire builders attempt to sabotage the influence and ministry of other leaders.

Given the opportunity, empire builders will attempt to destroy the influence of those they deem a threat to their own influence. Several years ago, I reunited with a key leader in another country after almost twelve years of disconnect. I tried numerous times to stay connected and could never understand why there was some kind of obstruction in our relationship. After speaking together for three hours it finally dawned on us that another leader who was jealous of my influence in this country had sabotaged our relationship because he wanted to supplant me as the covering of this key leader. I have also witnessed firsthand one leader insinuating lies about another key leader behind his back to try to stop his influence from spreading to other regions. In instances like these, we need to speak up and defend the honor of those not present in the room.

15. Empire builders tend to copy those they are jealous of in their region.

It is said that imitation is the highest form of flattery. Empire builders will appropriate and replicate the ideas of other leaders in their region and then attempt to outdo those same leaders. They may call it something different, but in the end it is essentially the same model but with an attitude to make it bigger and better than anything else in their region. It is like Dunkin' Donuts and McDonald's trying to reinvent themselves to keep up with Starbucks. Such an attitude is born out of personal competition rather than a pure love for Christ and His Kingdom.

16. Empire builders are narcissistic in relating to their desires in life.

Ultimately, empire builders are lovers of themselves. Thus, they will sacrifice the dreams and lives of others in order to fulfill their own dreams. They will throw everyone and anyone under the bus to advance their goals or to save their own skin. Their incredible commitment to the ministry is really only a commitment to advance their own ideals and dreams. This is pure narcissism, unlike the model of Christ, who laid down His own life for His sheep. Ezekiel chapter 34 gives a dire warning of the judgment God will bring on shepherds who use and abuse the sheep for their own pleasure.

17. Empire builders tell people that their church or network is the main key in their city for true revival and transformation.

When giving reports about their ministry, empire builders exaggerate the results of their work and utilize self-serving testimonies to back up their claims for spiritual dominance in their region. Many leaders have told me of prophecies they have received, alluding to the fact that it is their church that is going to start a revival for the nation or their community, or that revival is going to start in their region and go to the world because their region is the gate to the rest of the country.

I am presently cautiously optimistic when I hear of these prophecies; cautious because they often lead to justifying a myopic, self-focused vision, but optimistic because it is very possible for God to use one leader and/or church to catalyze a national revival.

Unfortunately, some prophetic leaders are motivated to give these flattering words to pastors so they will be invited back to preach; they know that many leaders fall prey to prophetic flattery. That being said, empire builders use these words, visions, and experiences to back up their claims that their particular church or ministry is "the church" in their region which God is going to use. This way, they can garner the loyalties of unsuspecting and naïve sheep and even pastors.

In my experience, most churches with this attitude are disciplined by God and actually begin to decline until their leaders repent of pride. Although it is possible that revival can come through one church to the whole world (e.g. the Azusa Street revival in 1906), this is the exception to the rule because community, city, and national transformation usually take place when God visits a region or nation and multitudes of churches receive "times of refreshing" all at the same time, resulting in the formation of informal apostolic networks that partner together to continue to perpetuate the advance of the Kingdom of God.

As we conclude this chapter, let me say that one of the things I think we in the church should consider is what Jesus said repeatedly in Revelation chapters 2 and 3: "He who has an ear, let him hear what the Spirit says to the churches" (Rev. 2:7, 11, 17, 29; 3:6, 13, 22). This profound statement says, in essence, that unless we are in unity with the Body of Christ in our region, many things God wants to say to the church will be limited. This is because in God's eyes, there is really only one church per city or community. The Spirit wants to speak to the churches, meaning that there are some things God will not speak to an individual believer or even an individual congregation. Biblically, there are many congregations but only one true church per community.

Consequently, praying with pastors representing our community or region releases God to communicate greater levels of His purpose and will. When we separate the Gospel from the Kingdom, we tend to build our own kingdoms and isolate ourselves from the rest of the body. This is because we are left only with "good news" for ourselves and our local congregation. When we connect the Gospel with the Kingdom, we recognize our obligation to see how we can work with other local congregations to manifest His Kingdom in our community and region.

Furthermore, when Jesus wanted to speak to the city church, He handed a letter to the "messenger" (bishop and/or apostle) of that city church. If Jesus wanted to say something to your city, who would He hand the letter to? If there is no unity and/or no apostolic alignment in your region. Who would convey the word of the Lord to the region?

Only when we connect the Gospel to the Kingdom do we have the theological pressure to partner with other members of the Body of Christ to manifest His Kingdom rather than build our own kingdom.

Chapter Fourteen

The church limited the Great Commission passages to individual redemption.

> *"And Jesus came and said to them, 'All authority in heaven and on earth has been given to me. Go therefore and make disciples of all nations, baptizing them in the name of the Father and of the Son and of the Holy Spirit, teaching them to observe all that I have commanded you. And behold, I am with you always, to the end of the age'" (Matthew 28:18-20).*

When I connected the Gospel to the Kingdom, one of the greatest things I discovered was that the "Great Commission" is not just about individual redemption but corporate redemption and transformation for nations (Matt. 28:19). Nation in the original language refers to groups of people, not individual ethnics. Also, Mark 16:15-18 shows that healing, deliverance, and speaking in new tongues can have a corporate interpretation. In other words, the church as a whole can bring healing to the peoples of a nation, not only through divine healing but also through the creation of institutions like hospitals. The church also can displace the power of evil principalities over a city, as we read in Luke 10:17. Furthermore, the church can supernaturally communicate the Gospel in the language of culture to reach a nation.

In addition, we see how the Great Commission as found in Mark has a focus on enlarging the family of God through evangelism and discipleship. The account in Matthew 28:19–20 refers to sending these disciples out to the surrounding culture to disciple their nation.

When we connect the Gospel to the Kingdom, we truly understand the importance of relating all key passages regarding our calling back to the original covenant of creation, which we referred to earlier in this book as the "Cultural Mandate" (Gen. 1:28). Mark's account of the Great Commission goes with the first part of the Cultural Mandate, which has to do with multiplying families for God, Matthew's account goes with the second half, dealing with sending saints into the world to disciple nations and thus transform culture.

In order to fulfill the Mark 16 component of the Great Commission, we need pastors, evangelists, and teachers to care for and equip the family of God. For the Matthew 28 account, we need apostles and prophets who act as bishops and generals to lead the advance of God's Kingdom on earth.

The following concepts come from a powerful teaching Dutch Sheets gave several years ago on the Ecclesia at the annual ICAL congress. (The original use of the Greek word *ecclesia* in history was to depict Roman/Greek citizens, assemblies, and/or Senators coming together to enact public policy. Jesus used this same word to depict His followers in Matthew 16:18, calling them to function as a congress or parliament under His rule as King of Kings.)

The enemy influenced the church to get rid of the function of apostles and prophets, which caused us to function merely as the family of God instead of as the family *and* army of God.

Without our focus on the Kingdom of God, the church will continue to sing while remaining (willfully?) oblivious to the surrounding culture. For example, during World War 2, while Jews were being herded to gas chambers by the Nazis, most churches in Germany ignored their cries and continued functioning as normal, conducting their worship services with little or no cultural engagement.

The world doesn't want us to practice the Kingdom; it wants us to function as the Sunday family of God—and nothing else.

Contrasting the Church and the Kingdom

We are not only family members of the Kingdom but also citizens of the Kingdom. Family has to do with our rights; Kingdom has to do with our responsibility as the Ecclesia.

- We are not only sheep and farmers but also judges.
- We are priests but also kings. Kings picture authority downward while priests function from the ground up.
- We are healers but also destroyers!
- We are ministers of the New Covenant but also legislators of the Covenant.
- We are those who apply the anointing oil for healing, but we also function as salt and light by preserving and enlightening the earth.
- In church we influence the family mountain; we need to influence the other mountains of culture as well.
- We can increase family until He comes, but we need also to increase the Kingdom until He comes. Success for us is both!

Have we done a good job in building local churches? Yes! Have we done a good job extending the culture of the Kingdom in our regions? No!

- In the church, Jesus saves; in the Kingdom, Jesus rules.
- In the church, we unite; in the Kingdom, we divide and conquer.
- In the church, we encourage; in the Kingdom, we command.
- When we function in the Kingdom, we are going to lead congregations that will listen to the leaders of the church the way the military does their generals.
- In the church, we minister; in the Kingdom, we commission people.
- In the church, we save individuals in the Kingdom, we disciple nations.
- In the church, we protect our family; in the Kingdom, we send them out in harm's way.

- In the church, we cast out demons; in the Kingdom, we dethrone demons from systems in society.
- In the church, the focus is care and relational; in the Kingdom, it is assignment and task.
- In the church, serving is encouraged for family; in the Kingdom, serving is mandatory for the King.
- In the church, the truth is encouraged and love abounds; in the Kingdom, the truth is mandatory to spread in every realm of society.
- In the church, individuality is encouraged; in the Kingdom, corporality is encouraged. (We must also ask ourselves "How do our congregations fit regionally with other congregations to affect our region"?)
- In the church, we gather and assemble; in the Kingdom, we disperse and send.
- In the church, happy, healthy family members are the goal; in the Kingdom, training good soldiers to take the lead is the goal.
- In the church, the local congregation is emphasized; in the Kingdom, the region is emphasized.
- In the church, we are called to shepherd our flock; in the Kingdom, we are called to shepherd whole communities.

If we don't get this we will have strong congregations but lose our culture!

- In the church, Jesus is our Friend; in the Kingdom, Jesus is also our Commander and King.
- In the church, love and compassion are emphasized along with the staff of the shepherd (Psalm 23); in the Kingdom, the scepter to rule is emphasized (Psalms 2 and 24).

As we conclude this chapter, my prayer is that we will understand the importance of connecting the Gospel to the Kingdom. If we do so, even our understanding of the Great Commission passages will be greatly enhanced!

Chapter Fifteen

Contrasting the Kingdom Mindset from the Religious Church Mindset

"But seek first the kingdom of God and his righteousness..." (Matthew 6:33)

As we come now to the final chapter in this book, I want to do a quick review of some of the basic premises we have discussed throughout.

Jesus, John the Baptist, and the apostles went about proclaiming the Kingdom of God, not the church (see Matt. 3:2; 4:17; 10:7; Acts 28:30-31). Although the church is in the Kingdom, it is not the entire Kingdom.

"Kingdom" denotes the rule of God over the whole cosmos, not just a single entity on the earth, like the church. In spite of this, most preaching today has as its goal to persuade people to make a weekly two-hour commitment to come to a building on Sundays and to give tithes to support that building! This is because a spirit of religion has captivated the church and blinded the minds of church leaders so that we now have a very limited church mindset instead of a Kingdom perspective. The negative results of this development cannot be overstated.

In essence, a Kingdom mindset regards Christianity as a biblical worldview and life philosophy centered on the person of Jesus Christ, who is Lord of all creation. This perspective has vast political, economic, and sociological implications!

Those with a church mindset view Jesus merely as the King of the church, not the King of all earthly, secular kings.

When we connect the Gospel to the Kingdom, we will have a different paradigm regarding the role of the believer and the nature of the church. When we view Scripture and the church through a Kingdom lens, it radically changes everything we have ever believed about our purpose and calling.

Contrasting the church and Kingdom mindsets

It is so important that we understand the difference between the typical church mindset and the Kingdom. I will attempt to make it as simple as possible with the following bullet points:

- A Kingdom mindset releases all saints as ministers in the marketplace. A church mindset merely trains people to serve in a church building on Sundays.
- A Kingdom mindset creates wealth to transform a community and/or a nation. A church mindset motivates giving to build our own church programs.
- A Kingdom mindset is a holistic approach that applies the Gospel to politics, economics, and public policy. A church mindset insulates the Gospel from politics and public policy.
- A Kingdom mindset views the Bible as a blueprint to structure every aspect of society. A church mindset views the Bible merely as a pietistic book that enables us to escape the world, enter heaven, and be spiritual.
- With a Kingdom mindset, churches embrace and love their surrounding unchurched communities. With a church mindset, churches only embrace converted individuals within their faith communities.
- A Kingdom mindset trains people for all of life. A church mindset trains people only for church life.
- A Kingdom mindset nurtures leaders who are world changers and "cultural creatives" who articulate truth to society. A church mindset nurtures leaders who speak religious language relevant only to church people.
- A Kingdom mindset speaks of the rule of God over the entire created order. A church mindset speaks of the

rule of God only through deacons and elders in their congregation.

- With a Kingdom mindset, pastors release their people to their vocational callings in the marketplace. A church mindset can (unintentionally) control people by marginalizing their marketplace callings and emphasizing only their Sunday ministries.
- A Kingdom mindset applies a Spirit-empowered approach to the natural world. A church mindset involves a spirituality that separates from the natural world.
- Those with a Kingdom mindset are working toward a renaissance of Christendom. Those with a church mindset merely strive for a particular expression (denomination) of Christianity.

Contrasting the Kingdom and a religious system

Jesus and the apostles did not inaugurate another religious system, but the age of the Kingdom of God. As we examine the gospels and the Book of Acts, we find that the main theme of the preaching was the Kingdom of God, not the church, and *definitely* not a religion.

The church is not the Kingdom, but the main agent of the Kingdom to represent God and manifest His government in the earth realm. In spite of this fact, many churches and denominations historically have bypassed Scripture and created a secondary tradition that is nowhere close to the way of Jesus and the apostles. I believe the time is presently at hand when God is shaking the global church and establishing Kingdom principles. God is ripping away extraneous second-tier traditions that are opposed to His Kingdom, irrespective of denominational affiliation. It is important for believers to understand the difference between characteristics of the Kingdom and those of religion. The world will only be transformed through the Kingdom of God.

Consider carefully the following contrasts between the Kingdom of God and a religious system:

- *In the Kingdom, the focus is on manifesting God in the earth; in religion, the focus is on applying their traditions inside church buildings.*

  Just the term "kingdom" implies both a king and his domain. Psalm 24:1 teaches us that the earth belongs to the Lord, and Psalm 22:28 says His kingdom rules over all nations, not just over the church. Consequently, we in His Kingdom (see Col. 1:12-13) are called to manifest His rule in the whole earth, not just the church realm.
- *In the Kingdom, an individual transforms from within; in religion, the focus is on observing outward rituals.*

  Jesus taught us in Matthew chapters 5-7 and 23 that God requires truth in the inner man (see also Ps. 51:6). Hence, the Kingdom focuses on inside-out transformation (see Lk. 17:21), while religion focuses primarily on observing rituals during church services.
- *In the Kingdom, all believers are released to the work of the ministry; in religion, only professional clergy are released to minister.*
- *In the Kingdom, all believers are both kings and priests (see Rom. 5:17; 1 Pet. 2:8-9). In religion, only those trained in seminary and who make a living in church ministry are called priests.*
- *In the Kingdom, the Spirit is poured out upon all flesh; in religion, the Spirit only moves during Sunday services.*

  The apostle Peter made it clear in Acts 2:17 that the resurrection inaugurated the Kingdom age in which the Holy Spirit was poured out upon every culture, tribe, kindred, tongue, and nation. He was not just for the religious Jews anymore, and His Spirit was no longer restricted to the Most Holy Place in their temple. In spite of this, many in the Body of Christ still believe the Holy Spirit only shows up within the four walls of a building during mass or church services.
- *In the Kingdom, the Scriptures have primary ecclesiastical authority; in religion, second tier religious tradition has primary ecclesial authority.*

This is an issue not only for the Roman Catholic Church, that puts tradition and canon law on equal terms with Scripture, and the Orthodox Church, in which many place the writings of the apostolic fathers on an equal level with the Holy Scriptures. Many evangelical protestant denominations (Pentecostal as well as non-Pentecostal) also have their own second-tier traditions that have primary authority regarding Christian practice.

- *In the Kingdom, the presence of God is wherever the believer goes; in religion, the presence of God is at the altar of their church building.*

  In the Kingdom, as shown in the gospels and the Book of Acts, the power and presence of God to heal, deliver, and save the oppressed was manifested more in the streets than in the synagogue or the temple. God wants to unleash an army of believers who will turn the world upside down, but religion wants to keep believers closeted inside church buildings.

- *In the Kingdom, the five-fold minister equips the saints to do the work of the ministry. In religion, the five-fold minister does all the work of the ministry.*

  In traditional religious systems, people are dependent upon professional clergy to pray for the sick, counsel, preach, and represent God to the world. In the Kingdom, five-fold ministry gifts are focused not on doing the work of the ministry but equipping the saints to do the work of the ministry (see Eph. 4:11-12).

- *In the Kingdom, the ministry focus is Monday through Friday; in religion, the ministry focus is Sunday.*

  Those participating in Kingdom-focused churches cannot wait until Monday; those trapped in religious systems only see purpose and meaning during church services.

- *In the Kingdom, the church is sent to serve their community; in religion, the church merely attempts to get the community into their church.*

In Kingdom-focused churches, believers are equipped to be the problem solvers of society. They are equipped with a biblical worldview to frame their service in every vocation that affects communities.

- *In the Kingdom, it is not merely about how many people attend the church services, but how many in the church are sent out to transform their world!*
- *In the Kingdom, the burden is for the whole Body of Christ; in religion, the burden is for their own denomination and local church.*

  Any person or leader with a Kingdom agenda will have a concern for the health of the whole Body of Christ, irrespective of their denomination. Those with a religious mindset are sectarian and only care about the health of their own denomination and/or church.
- *In the Kingdom, every believer is a priest; in religion, only the professional clergy serve as priests.*
- *In the Kingdom, every sphere of life is integrated under King Jesus; in religion, the church stays out of the public square.*

  The Kingdom of God integrates the rule of God with societal structures such as law, politics, economics, families, art, and business. In religion, politics and economics are unspiritual and should be left to the world.
- *In the Kingdom, Jesus is the King of kings; in religion, He is merely the symbolic leader of the church.*
- *In the Kingdom, Jesus is not only the head of the church but the King of kings (see Rev. 19:16).*

  This is the most politically charged statement anyone can make about Jesus! It means Jesus is the political head of every president and politician, as well as the governor of every governor and the mayor of every mayor. This obligates every believer to be politically active by voting and doing their part to speak truth to power, as well as promote candidates who best represent Kingdom values.
- *In the Kingdom, the church is the salt of the earth; in religion, the believer is the salt of the church.*

Jesus called His followers the salt of the earth and the light of the world, not the salt of the church and the light of their religion.

- *In the Kingdom, the focus is on transforming the earth; in religion, the focus is on perpetuating its traditions in the church.*
- *In the Kingdom, culture is engaged; in religion, disengagement and escape from the earth are desired.*

  The nature of religion is that it wants to create its own enclave of safety from the unpredictable realities of the unredeemed world. Religion is mystical, not practical or spiritual. However, those trained in the Kingdom view every earthly challenge as an opportunity to be a problem solver and to bring Christ into culture.
- *The Kingdom is relational; religion is hierarchical.*

  The Kingdom of God is built upon relationships, not church ministry. Conversely, religious systems are primarily hierarchical and built upon titles and positions. This causes much political unrest and competition within the denomination because esteem is conferred upon individuals based upon how high one is stationed on the titular totem pole.

***

May God help all of us discern whether we are primarily informed by the Kingdom or by a religious tradition and system.

Additional teachings and resources by Dr. Joseph Mattera, can be found at

www.josephmattera.org

Audio

https://soundcloud.com/josephmattera

Other books by Joseph Mattera – Available for purchase on Amazon

Kingdom Revolution

Kingdom Awakening

Ruling In The Gates

Walk In Generational Blessings

Understanding The Wineskin of the Kingdom

An Anthology of Essays on Apostolic Leadership

Essays on Cutting Edge Leadership

Travail to Prevail

25 Truths You Never Heard in Church

Connect with
Dr. Joseph Mattera at any of the following locations:

740 40TH STREET
BROOKLYN NY 11232, USA
718.436.0242 EXT. 13
INFO@JOSEPHMATTERA.ORG

Facebook: /josephmattera
Twitter: /josephmattera
YouTube: /josephmattera
Instagram: /joseph_mattera

Powered by eGenCo

Generation Culture Transformation
Specializing in publishing for generation culture change

Visit us Online at:
www.micro65.com

Write to: eGenco
824 Tallow Hill Road
Chambersburg, PA 17202, USA
Phone: 717-461-3436
Email: info@micro65.com

facebook.com/egenbooks
youtube.com/egenpub
egen.co/blog
pinterest.com/eGenDMP
twitter.com/egen_co
instagram.com/egen.co

Made in the USA
Middletown, DE
11 May 2019